ELEVATE

ELEVATE
A 52-Week Encounter with God

ROB MCCORKLE

FSM  PUBLISHING | Groveport, OH

Fire School Ministries
P.O. Box 511
Groveport, OH 43125
fireschoolministries.com

© 2018 by Rob McCorkle

All rights reserved solely by the author. The author guarantees all contents are original and do not infringe upon the legal rights of any other person or work. No part of this book may be reproduced in any form without the permission of the author. The views expressed in this book are not necessarily those of the publisher.

Unless otherwise indicated, Scripture quotations taken from the New American Standard Bible (NASB). Copyright © 1960, 1962, 1963, 1968, 1971, 1972, 1973, 1975, 1977, 1995 by The Lockman Foundation. Used by permission. All rights reserved.

Many of the Greek definitions are taken from Rick Renner, *Sparkling Gems from the Greek* (Tulsa, OK: Teach All Nations, 2003), Rick Meyer, e-Sword, www.e-sword.net/downloads.html, and Logos Bible Software 5.

Cover design by Nate Braxton.
nbraxton@gmail.com

Printed in the United States of America.

ISBN-13: 9781545644119

Acknowledgements

I'm grateful for the tenacious work of my youngest son, Jesse, and our graphic artist Nate Braxton.

I'm grateful for the hours of work that Karen Stout, Fire School's administrator, has put into this small book.

I'm grateful for my wife who labors so diligently at our church so that I may labor on the road, preaching in churches and writing books in hotel rooms.

Finally, I'm most grateful for the lessons that the Lord is teaching me. You are reading a few of those lessons.

Table of Contents

Acknowledgements vii
Introduction xiii

1. The More Excellent Way 1
2. The Suffering in Love 7
3. The Impartation of Love .12
4. The Danger of Grumbling. 17
5. Words. 23
6. Being a Worshiper 29
7. Releasing His Presence 34
8. Perseverance. 39
9. Never Quit. 44
10. Lower and Slower 49
11. Sustaining the Fire 54
12. Don't Be Led Astray. 59
13. Greater Than You Think .64
14. Doing What Jesus Did. 69
15. The One Thing 74
16. Borderless Faith (Part One). 79
17. Borderless Faith (Part Two) 84
18. Believe, Then Speak. 89

19. No Shrinking Back 94
20. Word Versus Circumstances 99
21. Living with a Kingdom Mindset 104
22. The Power of Hearing 110
23. Dull of Hearing. 115
24. Holiness. 120
25. Revelation into Revelation 125
26. Faith and Patience 130
27. The Sword of the Spirit 136
28. Life in the Spirit 141
29. Being Led by the Spirit 146
30. Quenching the Spirit 151
31. Grieving the Spirit 156
32. Dove or Pigeon. 161
33. Unaware of His Presence 167
34. Leaders or Followers 172
35. Revival Is Messy. 177
36. Academics Versus Anointing 183
37. A Prophetic Lifestyle 189
38. Greater Manifestations of the Spirit 194
39. A Spirit of Revelation. 199
40. Dying to Live 204
41. Houses of Prayer 209
42. The Faith to Pray 215
43. The Breath of Intercession. 221
44. Destroying Strongholds 226
45. Breaking the Power of Offense. 231
46. Forgiveness 237
47. Breaking an Orphan Mindset. .242
48. Extraordinary Power 248

Table of Contents

49. Stagnant or Fresh 253
50. Trusting the Word 258
51. Resting in the Storm 263
52. Believing Beyond Criticism 268

Other Books by Rob McCorkle..................... 273
Notes 275

Introduction

The book of Revelation is an unveiling of truth given to a disciple of Christ who yielded to an invitation by God. John was given an opportunity to "come up" to where the Lord was and to learn things from His perspective. The result of John's willingness was his opportunity to see and hear spectacular things. While John's encounter was unique, we have been given an opportunity to see and hear profound truths as well. The Bible tells us to "seek the things that are above, where Christ is, seated at the right hand of God" (Colossians 3:1a). This is an invitation to all of us to raise our thinking, viewpoints, attitude, and lives to a heavenly perspective.

Elevate contains fifty-two devotionals that are designed to help you seek those things that are above. There are two things that mean so very much to me. First, I thoroughly love the Word of God. The Bible is alive! It's been brought into existence by the very breath of God, and it has the inspirational ability to adequately equip you for every assignment God gives. I trust the Word and believe that every page of the Word of God is accurate and without error. Each devotional will contain several Scriptures and, in some cases, many references.

Additionally, I love the meaning of words. Yes, I'm a word nerd and, as a result, you will often find key words defined in such a manner that will clarify the meaning for you, making the Bible easier to understand. I hope that this will be a blessing to you and that you will gain a deeper appreciation for the Scriptures and their relevancy to your life.

Secondly, I deeply value the presence of the Holy Spirit. Our greatest teacher is the Spirit of truth because He discloses kingdom secrets from the Father. In fact, He searches the deep things of God and then freely shares them with you through revelation, insight, and guidance. The Holy Spirit enables us to fulfill the mandates of the Word. He empowers, inspires, and anoints us to do the impossible and to live the unthinkable. We are abundantly blessed because we have the Holy Spirit within.

I believe that the Word and the Spirit are inseparable. And I believe that as you journey through these lessons you are going to encounter the unchanging, timeless truths of the Word and that you are going to encounter the manifest presence of the Holy Spirit. My life and ministry will be forever changed by the fusion of the Word and Spirit in my life, and I believe the same for you. My prayer is that you'll be elevated to new places in your spiritual walk through this book. May we all *come up* to a kingdom perspective, and may we all be shaped by what we see and hear from the Lord.

Rob McCorkle
May 14, 2018

1
The More Excellent Way

When you truly love, it is impossible for you to feel hurt or let down by the recipients of your love.

What is the more excellent way to live?

The Bible states the following about love: Love is the greatest commandment (Matthew 22:37-39), love is the distinguishing characteristic of being Jesus' follower (John 13:35), love is the sweet-smelling fragrance of Christ (Ephesians 5:2), love is the bond of perfection (Colossians 3:14), and love never fails (1 Corinthians 13:8). After Paul described a supernatural culture where the Holy Spirit manifested for the profit of the entire body of Christ, he transitioned into a chapter that has affectionately been called the "love chapter."

In 1 Corinthians 12:31, Paul began his discourse as he wrote to the Corinthians that he was going to "show [them] a still more excellent way." Suffice to say that the "more excellent way" that Paul talked about was a description of something that is beyond comparison or beyond measure. It was not a lifestyle void of the supernatural gifts but rather a supernatural lifestyle expressed in the most excellent way. If the manifestations of the Spirit are going to make the greatest impact, they must flow from a person who is becoming love.

Years ago, a scholar named W. T. Purkiser observed that the grammar in Galatians 5:22 argued for *one* central fruit of the Spirit. The word fruit (*karpos*) is a singular noun, and the verse indicates that the fruit of the Spirit *is,* implying that only one fruit emerges in a person's life when filled with the Spirit. The remaining eight characteristics, then, spill out of a person who is walking in love. S. D. Gordon once suggested the following:[1]

- Joy is love singing
- Peace is love resting
- Patience is love enduring
- Faithfulness is love's habit
- Kindness is love sharing
- Goodness is love's character
- Gentleness is love's touch
- Self-control is love in charge

What *is* love? How is it defined? You need to realize that the term is washed out in our culture because we say things like "I love my wife" and "I love my dog" and hopefully in that order, too. But what does it mean to love? Unlike the English language, which has only one word for "love," the Greek language has four different words. First, is the word *eros,* which is defined as a sexual, erotic type of love. However, this word is never used in the Bible, not even in the context of sexual intimacy between a husband and wife. The root idea behind this word is selfish gratification, and it's far from what God calls us to.

Second is the word *stergo,* which is a relational love as seen in a family. It's used rarely in the Bible, and where we find this type of love, it's depicted in a negative manner. For example, in 2 Timothy 3:3, *stergo* is defined as being unloving. Third is the word *phileo,* which describes the affection between two people. This word is used several places in the New Testament, and usually it depicts the love between friends. *Phileo* is usually used as a compound word that describes the love of something specific, for example: the love of our brother (*philadelphia*), the love of wisdom (*philosophia*), or the love of strangers (*philoxenos*).

The final word is *agape,* and this word, which is used in the New Testament, defines the love of God. This type of love is only generated by God. It defines who God is: 1 John 4:8 says that He is love (*agape*). We cannot actuate this kind of love without being filled with God's Spirit. There is no way to manufacture *agape* through our own efforts. We experience His love first, and then He enables us to give it away to others.

Over the years I've read many definitions of this kind of love, but no definition has touched me more than Rick Renner's description. He wrote, "Such great respect is awakened in the heart of the observer for the person he is beholding that he is compelled to love them. In fact, his love for that person is so strong that it is irresistible. . . . when you love with this kind of love, it is impossible for you to feel hurt or let down by the response of the recipients of your love."[2]

Think about that for a moment. Do you get hurt by people who don't treat you well? Are you easily offended by someone who says or does something to hurt you? Perhaps you really don't love them with *agape* love. This kind of love is not contingent upon others responding favorably toward you. If you truly love someone with *agape* love, you aren't seeking anything from them. Your only thought is to pour love upon them because you have been radically transformed by the love of God. Your heart is engaged in giving no matter how you're treated. You are simply compelled to love others.

After three years of pouring His life out for others, the very people that Jesus touched, healed, cleansed, and cured turned on Him and crucified Him. Yet, Jesus didn't retaliate in offense. We can't even imagine Jesus getting halfway to the cross and stopping to say, "Barabbas? Are you serious? You want Barabbas instead of me? That is so totally unfair." If we can't imagine Jesus saying something like that, then what is our excuse?

Jesus forgave the angry mobs because He loved them and because He realized that they had no idea what they were doing. That response is the nature of *agape* love, and it compels us to lay down our lives for other people regardless of what they say or do to us. You simply love others — no questions, no expectations, no reservations, or no strings attached. Because God has loved you, you are enabled to love others, and because God's love is unlimited, your love for others reflects that same characteristic.

In some ways, nothing is more miraculous than *agape* love. When you love with His love, you become impervious to the ill effects of other people. Why? Because to truly love with *agape* love, you are dead! In other words, your life has been crucified with Christ, and He lives through you (Galatians 2:20). So, you give, you pray, you sacrifice, you forgive, you heal, you minister, and you simply don't think of yourself anymore. Your life is a funnel that God's incredible love is poured through.

This kind of love changed our world two-thousand years ago when Jesus declared, "It is finished" (John 19:30). We have the blessed privilege to extend that same kind of love all over our world. Open your heart to Jesus right now: experience His love in your life and then become His instrument to touch the lives of everyone you meet with His amazing love. This is the more excellent way.

PRAYER

Jesus, with the help of your Holy Spirit, enable me to become love. I realize that this is the more excellent way to live, amen.

APPLICATION

1. How would you define love?
2. Can you identify five people who walk the more excellent way?
3. What would your life look like if you walked every day in *agape* love?
4. What are some things that hinder *agape* love from being consistently lived out?
5. Have you truly died to yourself? Ask the Lord to crucify your flesh and love through you.

2

The Suffering in Love

Our call is to demonstrate love to a fallen world, but keep in mind that those whom we love will often be incapable of returning agape love.

Did you know that if you truly love someone, then you might suffer?

Sometimes nothing sets you up to suffer more than when you really love someone, especially someone who doesn't reciprocate your love for them. In Lesson One, we dealt with the subject matter of *agape* love, in this lesson I want to continue with that same thought. This kind of love describes God because God is *agape* (1 John 4:8). Love such as this is sacrificial in nature. Rick Renner said, "When you love with this kind of love, it is impossible for you to feel hurt or let down by the response of the recipients of your love."[3]

True love is never about you, and if we have the same attitude in us that was also in Jesus, then we will give our lives away to others just as He did (Philippians 2:5-8). This particular passage in Philippians has been called "the emptying" because Jesus "emptied" (*kenoo*) Himself, taking on the form of a servant, and gave Himself to us (Philippians 2:7). Jesus loved you and me regardless of our willingness to return His love: He was compelled to love us.

Jesus commissioned us to love others in like manner. He said, "But I say to you, love your enemies and pray for those who persecute you" (Matthew 5:44). Think about that for a moment. He told us to love our *enemies*! The word "enemies" describes those who are hostile toward God and people. These people oppose us, and they oppose what is right, godly, and decent. Jesus loved people who were incapable of reciprocating His love. They were sinful: they were "by nature children of wrath" (Ephesians 2:3). All of us were in the same condition. We were all filled with sin and incapable of loving God or people with *agape*. Yet, He loved us anyway, and His love made a way for us to be redeemed from sin.

Our call is to demonstrate this exact love to a fallen world, but keep in mind that those whom we love will often be incapable of returning *agape* love. Moreover, I would argue that even in churches people have skewed understandings of real love. So, when you love someone who persecutes you, who maligns your character, or who takes advantage of you, you will suffer because you are giving something away that isn't being returned. But *agape* love doesn't think about "self." This love enables you to love without being offended (trapped by the hurt). Like Jesus, you have been emptied of everything and filled with the Holy Spirit. Becoming love,

The Suffering in Love

then, is who you are: you *are* love because you are filled with the essence of God.

Jesus added more insight to this idea of loving others in Luke 6:27b where he says, "Do good to those who hate you." We're not to retaliate, gossip, complain, or vent our frustration on Facebook, but rather we have been commanded to "do good" to those who hate us. Jesus demonstrated that kind of lifestyle for us: "But emptied Himself, taking on the form of a bond-servant, and being made in the likeness of men. Being found in appearance as a man, He humbled Himself by becoming obedient to the point of death, even death on a cross" (Philippians 2:7–8).

Jesus descended lower, so He made it possible for you and me to experience the love of God and to be set free from our sin. Our attitude is to be the same (Philippians 2:5). Our call is to lower ourselves like He did. It is to go low enough so that it makes it possible for others to experience the love of Christ through us. This is how we touch our world for God. Most people will not listen to a message if the messenger isn't demonstrating love. Love never fails (1 Corinthians 13:8), especially when we speak the truth *in love* (Ephesians 4:15).

A friend of mine told me about a ministry group that was attacked by natives while conducting a Christian service in a remote part of Africa. Most of the group managed to get to the safety of their vehicles and escape without severe injuries. One person, however, stepped in to take the full brunt of pain so that the others could escape. They beat this person almost senseless. When the police captured the perpetrators, they wanted to know if this ministry group would press charges. The group decided not to, but the man who had been beat asked to spend a few moments with the angry mob. His love for his abusers was too much for them to withstand. They were compelled to know the love of God that would enable a persecuted man to extend forgiveness as he did. That sounds a lot like Jesus, doesn't it?

I have miles to go when it comes to loving people like Jesus does. I'm not sure that I would have responded in the same manner as the man in the story above, but I sure want to. I want to repent for anything that isn't like Jesus, and I want to empty myself of everything but love. I want the same attitude as Jesus.

What about you? Are you compelled by love (2 Corinthians 5:14)? If we love others, then we will never adjust our attitude based on what people do to us because our attitude has been aligned with Christ's image. Jesus descended into greatness. We only rise higher by going lower, by humbling ourselves and loving others regardless of how we're treated. That is a challenge, but with the help of the Holy Spirit we can live in love.

The Suffering in Love

PRAYER

Jesus, love never fails. I repent of everything in me that isn't like you. I ask that you will cleanse my heart and fill me with your Holy Spirit. Enable me to love. Love through me, and touch others with your love, amen.

APPLICATION

1. Are you challenged to love someone who doesn't treat you very well?
2. Have you, or someone that you know, undergone persecution?
3. How did you or the other person respond?
4. What can you do, with the help of the Holy Spirit, so that you're not offended?
5. What are some practical ways to go lower like Jesus did?

3
The Impartation of Love

Love looks upward and outward. It remains focused on Jesus, which then enables us to truly see other people.

I've been so blessed these days as I observe people being touched by the presence of God. Over the last few years, I have personally witnessed hundreds of miracles. It has led to an even greater hunger for the outpouring of the Holy Spirit. In almost every meeting that I lead, I usually close our time together with an impartation.

In Romans 1:11, Paul wrote, "For I long to see you so that I may impart some spiritual gift to you, that you may be established." The verb impart (*metadidimi*) means to give something over to someone else or to place upon another person something that you possess. Paul was referring to a supernatural gift in this verse, believing that it would be established in these Christians in Rome.

I believe in the ministry of impartation because it is biblical (1 Timothy 4:14; 2 Timothy 1:6). Additionally, I've seen the fruit of this ministry through the impartations I've received and from those I've given. There is always an increase of power and a greater release of the gifts when impartations are given and received. But there is something even greater than power, gifts, and anointing that we can impart, and that is the impartation of God's love.

Without love, our messages are nothing more than noisy gongs and clanging cymbals (1 Corinthians 13:1). If we're not imparting love, our ministry gifts and supernatural manifestations profit absolutely nothing (1 Corinthians 13:2-3). Recently, I was looking over the infamous "love chapter" in 1 Corinthians chapter 13. Paul described what love is, what it's not, and what it does. Then he concluded his description with this phrase: "Love never fails" (1 Corinthians 13:8).

Think about that for a moment. Messages may fail, ministry events may fail, outreach attempts may fail, and even churches may fail. But if our activity is being prompted and inspired by divine love, we leave a heavenly residue of eternal substance.

Love, biblical love (*agape*), cannot be generated by human effort. In fact, if God's love is going to manifest in our lives, it requires that we "get out of the way." In other words, we must die to ourselves so that Jesus can live through us (Galatians 2:20). Stated differently, if we are full of ourselves, then we cannot be full of God.

The Bible says in Philippians 2:5-7, "Have this attitude in yourselves which was also in Jesus Christ, who, although He existed in the form of God, did not regard equality with God a thing to be grasped, but emptied Himself, taking the form of a bond-servant, *and* being made in the likeness of men." Jesus emptied Himself! He descended from the form of God to the form of a slave. His equality with God was exchanged for the equality of a human being. Therefore, He was subject to all temptations just like we experience, yet He was without sin (Hebrews 4:15).

The challenge of this passage in Philippians is the admonition to have the same attitude as Jesus did. Out of love, Jesus descended even to the point of dying for people who were still sinners (Romans 5:8). Jesus' love for the Father and for mankind compelled Him to the cross. "Greater love has no one than this, that one lay down his life for his friends" (John 15:13). Jesus not only laid down His life for friends but for His enemies, too. Does this describe your attitude?

After Jesus stripped off His robe and washed the disciples' feet, He spoke to them about a new commandment. That commandment was to love others to the same degree that Jesus loved others. This kind of love, Jesus said, would become the distinguishing characteristic of being His follower (John 13:34–35). But it requires a willingness to lay down our lives for Jesus (John 13:38), and that's a tall order for many people.

Love is tangible and practical—let me explain. I boarded a plane one time with headphones over my ears. When I landed, the Lord finally pierced through the music that I was listening to, and He explained how "unloving" I was to the person beside me. My unspoken message to the person sitting beside me on that particular flight was that they were of no concern to me. Please, listen to music if you want, but listen first to the voice of the Holy Spirit. Perhaps He wants to say something through you to people around you. When you walk in love, people are not interruptions, but rather they are opportunities to give Jesus away. You will never look into the eyes of someone who doesn't matter to Jesus.

Love looks upward and outward. It remains focused on Jesus which then enables us to truly see other people. Love empowers us to look into people's hearts, to pay attention when they're speaking, and to be moved with compassion for them. Love affects the way we speak to people around us, including our spouse, children, and grandchildren. Love is approachable and nonthreatening, too. People will be drawn to us because they sense divine love. This kind of love will pour into others without being noticed for its deeds. There is a gentleness to love that welcomes everyone regardless of who they are. Love will embrace truth without being abrasive, and it will draw the best out in others without flattery and deceit.

The Bible says to be imitators of God (Ephesians 5:1). How can we mimic God? We do so by "walking in love" just like Jesus did (Ephesians 5:2). God is love, so to be like God *is* to be love. One of my greatest desires is to deposit love wherever I walk. I want to be known as a lover of God and people. My challenge to you is to become love and give it away to all you meet.

PRAYER

I choose to die to myself so that you can live through me, Jesus. May my life become love to everyone who I am around, amen.

APPLICATION

1. Do you believe that you are filled with the love of God? Why or why not?
2. When you are around people, would they be touched by the love that is in you?
3. What are some tangible ways you have walked in love recently?
4. What are some ways that love can increase in your life?

4

The Danger of Grumbling

If God brought leprosy upon those who complained today, what would be the condition of our lives? Maybe some of our churches are dying because we grumble against the leadership, finances, facility, music, or its people.

Not long ago, I was studying a passage of Scripture that challenged me in regard to the kinds of things that come out of my mouth. Have you ever considered the words that you speak? Jesus indicated that our words are so significant that they could actually condemn us (Matthew 12:37). Paul wrote saying that we are never to speak a fruitless word to another person (Ephesians 4:29), and elsewhere he stated that every word we speak should be filled with grace and seasoned with salt (Colossians 4:6).

Jesus said, "It is the Spirit who gives life; the flesh profits nothing; the words that I have spoken to you are spirit and are life" (John 6:63). Think about that statement: every word that Jesus spoke contained life. He spoke only as the Father prompted Him according to John 12:50; therefore, not one time did He ever speak in the flesh. That would mean that Jesus never grumbled or complained because grumbling, by its very definition, is words uttered in the flesh.

There's an interesting passage that underscores the importance of not grumbling. Paul clearly stated that this passage was "written for our instruction" (1 Corinthians 10:11). He referenced the Israelites who had experienced a number of supernatural occurrences while journeying through the wilderness. He wrote about them eating supernatural food, drinking supernatural water, and using a fountain that was a supernatural rock—which represented Christ.

However, in spite of these incredible experiences, the Israelites were dispersed and scattered in the desert because of the specific sins that they committed. Paul identified the first three sins that, to me, are no doubt serious enough to evoke God's wrath. They were idolatry, immorality, and testing the Lord (1 Corinthians 10:7-9). But the fourth sin is what caught my attention. Paul wrote, "Nor grumble, as some of them did, and were destroyed by the destroyer" (1 Corinthians 10:10).

Grumbling? Are you serious? We grumble about the weather, economy, politics, church leadership, and even traffic during the holidays. Someone recently complained that they weren't able to find a parking spot at the mall. Grumbling is a way of life for many of us. But I want to propose to you that it is a serious sin that aligns us to the work of darkness, and it was a costly sin for the Israelites that should warn every one of us.

The Danger of Grumbling

The word grumble (*gongyzo*) means to murmur or speak complaints under your breath against someone or something. One expositor stated that grumbling comes from our agreement with something that is always contrary to God's will. It's a symptom of faithlessness, and so our mouth declares our agreement with hopelessness. Given the fact that our mouths contain life and death (Proverbs 18:21), our complaints become negative prophecies over our lives and situations.

Miriam and Aaron, in a sense, complained and grumbled against Moses (Numbers 12:1-10). The Bible indicates that Miriam was a prophetess (Exodus 15:20). Therefore, she was prophesying against an appointed leader and God heard her complaints—He always hears what we say. God's anger burned against Miriam and Aaron, the priest and prophet, and Miriam's skin turned leprous.

We might question what happens to the body of Christ when churches are filled with grumbling, complaining members. If God brought leprosy upon those who complained today, what would be the condition of our lives? Maybe some of our churches are dying because we grumble against the leadership, finances, facility, music, or its people.

Much of our grumbling isn't even being whispered anymore. These days complaints are posted all over Facebook and the Internet for others to commiserate with. It's appalling to read what believers write about in regard to other people, churches, and leaders. Much of the complaining and negative speech is fruitless and barren words that one day we will be held accountable for.

Because of grumbling, the Israelites "were destroyed by the destroyer" (1 Corinthians 10:10). The word destroyer (*olothreutes*) refers to a venomous snake. A similar word appears in Exodus 12:23 referring to the death angel sent to smite those not covered by the blood. The Israelites' grumbling was so serious to God that it severed their covenant with Him. Therefore, they were spiritually uncovered and became vulnerable to the enemy. Their complaints aligned them with a spirit of death. Think about this: your words indicate with whom or what you are aligning yourself.

Paul wrote, "Do all things without grumbling or disputing; so that you will prove yourselves to be blameless and innocent, children of God above reproach in the midst of a crooked and perverse generation, among whom you appear as lights in the world" (Philippians 2:14-15). One of the ways that we prove ourselves to be blameless and innocent is by doing things without grumbling. God desires that we live above reproach amidst a perverse generation. That means we are to speak words of life no matter what we are doing. Paul continued to write that we were to hold fast to the "word of life" (Philippians 2:16). Perhaps holding to the "word of life" is speaking words of life every time that you talk.

I believe that our mouths speak what our hearts are full of (Matthew 12:34). Therefore, if we are full of the Holy Spirit and filled with His Word, then our mouths will release content that manifests truth and life. Let God sanctify your tongue today and ask the Holy Spirit to cleanse and fill you. Ask the Holy Spirit to guard your mouth so that every word

The Danger of Grumbling

you speak is life. Fill your heart and mind with the Word so that when you are squeezed and agitated, His Word spills from your lips rather than grumbling.

PRAYER

God, I want a mouth that never grumbles or complains. Cleanse my heart and fill me with your Spirit. May I learn to stuff myself with your Word so that I may speak as Jesus did with words that are spirit and life, amen.

APPLICATION

1. Take an inventory of the words that come out of your mouth: Do you grumble and complain?
2. If you do complain, what are the reasons for it?
3. How do you feel when you are around someone who is negative and complaining?
4. What would your life look like if you never complained?
5. Here's a challenge: Would you be willing to participate in a "grumble fast" for three months?

5
Words

Careless words have split churches, wounded pastors, and impeded the progress of the kingdom of God. And in the final analysis, Jesus said we will either be justified or condemned by our words.

Do you know what the most destructive weapon is?

We've all heard about "weapons of mass destruction," but, in reality, the most devastating weapon known to humanity is our tongue. In the epistle of James, we're told that a human being does not have the power or ability (apart from Christ) to tame the tongue. In fact, James calls the tongue a "restless" evil (James 3:8)—a word used only here in the New Testament to describe something that is unrestrainable, unstable, and prone to great harm. James says that the tongue is "full of deadly poison" (James 3:8).

Poison (*ios*) describes venom that is emitted from a snake that paralyzes their prey so that the snake can consume them.

Interestingly, your words can immobilize another person, rendering them easy prey for the enemy to destroy. Words have the ability to wound, injure, scar, and destroy another human being.

The Proverbs are filled with challenges about the tongue. We are told that the tongue:
1. Conceals violence (10:11).
2. Brings ruination (10:14).
3. Destroys neighbors (11:9).
4. Tears down cities (11:11).
5. Stirs up anger (15:1).
6. Spouts folly (15:2).
7. Crushes the spirit (15:4).
8. Brings strife (18:6).
9. Snares our soul (18:7).

Proverbs 18:21a says, "Death and life are in the power of the tongue,..." By your words, you can declare that dry bones live again (Ezekiel 37:7–10), or you can burn a great forest to the ground (James 3:5–6). Paul wrote, "Let no unwholesome word proceed from your mouth, . . ." (Ephesians 4:29a).

Unwholesome (*sapros*) describes something that is rotten, useless, or corrupted. One expositor said it refers to a word that is barren and lifeless—a word spoken in the flesh and not anointed by the Holy Spirit. Unwholesome words are similar to "empty words" in Ephesians 5:6, and Paul indicated that the wrath of God comes upon those who deceive others with them. Keep in mind that these unfruitful words can be written in e-mails, texts, Facebook, and Twitter, not merely spoken.

I have never ceased to be amazed by how careless believers are with their words. Proverbs 10:19a says, "When there are many words, transgression is unavoidable, . . ." I've observed believers exaggerate the truth, attempt to impress, flatter, misalign, and slander the character of others with words. I've had hurtful and untrue words written about me, my family, and my church. I've heard unkind words spoken about other churches, pastors, leaders, and denominations.

I've heard hateful words spoken in haste toward different ethnic groups, political candidates, and world leaders. It's unbecoming of Spirit-filled believers. Careless words have split churches, wounded pastors, and impeded the progress of the kingdom of God. And in the final analysis, Jesus said we will either be justified or condemned by our words (Matthew 12:37).

There is only one way the tongue can be tamed: we must die to ourselves and allow the Holy Spirit to possess us. Then, moment by moment, we must walk in the Spirit (Galatians 5:25). Jesus is our example of walking in the Spirit and speaking under heaven's influence. In fact, Jesus *only* said what the Father told Him (John 12:50). That's why all of Jesus' words were filled with the Spirit and life (John 6:63).

Jesus' words were so anointed that when He spoke, demons fled, nature obeyed, elements transformed, disease dissipated, crippled limbs straightened, and dead bodies were restored. Jesus said, "A pupil is not above his teacher; but everyone, after he has been fully trained, will be like his teacher" (Luke 6:40). If Jesus only spoke under the power of heaven, then it's possible for you and me to do the same. The New Testament believers spoke "as the Spirit was giving them utterance" (Acts 2:4b). They spoke with power and boldness because their tongues were under the influence of the Holy Spirit. What would happen if you only spoke as the Spirit gave you utterance?

If we'll remain in the Spirit, our words can impart grace to others (Ephesians 4:29). Paul said, "Let your speech always be with grace, as *though* seasoned with salt, so that you will know how you should respond to each person" (Colossians 4:6). Proverbs 10 identifies some benefits of the tongue if we'll remain in the Spirit.

1. The mouth of the righteous is a fountain of life (v. 11).
2. On the lips of the discerning, wisdom is found (v. 13).
3. The tongue of the righteous is as choice silver (v. 20).
4. The lips of the righteous feed many (v. 21).
5. The mouth of the righteous flows with wisdom (v. 31).
6. The lips of the righteous bring forth what is acceptable (v. 32).

Proverbs 11:11a says, "By the blessing of the upright a city is exalted, . . ." Speak blessings over your city. Don't let the culture define what your city will be but declare what your city can be under the influence of the Holy Spirit. I don't want to speak negative statements over my city and pronounce curses. I believe that gives the enemy a legal right to attach himself to my flesh-filled pronouncements. Instead, I want my city to be exalted under the power of the Lord God Most High. What about your city?

I want to speak the right words over people, too. Rather than define who people are, I want to declare what they're going to be under the transforming power of God. Let's be people who "calls into being that which does not exist" (Romans 4:17b). Let's become people whose words are influenced by a spirit of faith, as 2 Corinthians 4:13b says, "... We also believe, therefore we also speak." Additionally, if we'll remain in the Spirit, then our mouths can speak prophetically into the hearts of those around us. Our Spirit-inspired words will edify, exhort, and comfort those we speak into (1 Corinthians 14:3).

PRAYER

Jesus, possess my mouth. Cleanse my tongue from lifeless words. Enable me to speak only under the influence of your Spirit, amen.

APPLICATION

1. Over the past month, have words of life or death come out of your mouth?
2. Do you have a problem with an untamed tongue? If so, what are the reasons for that?
3. What would it look like if you *only* spoke words of life? Would it change some of your relationships?
4. How many Proverbs have you found that address the subject of the tongue, the mouth, and our lips?

6

Being a Worshiper

True worship is an increasing affection for God that showers praise and thanksgiving to Him in every moment of our lives regardless of what we walk through.

I remember a particular service at our church when I stopped the singing. There was nothing wrong with the song we were singing, but there was apathy in our response toward God that day that was almost oppressive. When I stood up and looked out over the crowd, I saw people on their phones. Others were sitting with their arms folded, and still others stood singing with little to no passion. Perhaps a few were engaged in *true* worship that day, but the vast majority in the crowd that day was unmoved, unresponsive, distracted, and disengaged.

I wonder how many churches are filled with disengaged worship. Has worship in our churches become a religious activity or lifeless ritual that we merely do to fill time until we get to the sermon? And what *is* worship? For some, worship is singing a hymn. Others prefer southern gospel. Throughout the '70s and '80s, we were inundated with choruses. However, the church that I grew up in was careful not to get too emotional lest we be like the "charismatics."

For some, worship is *only* singing. Others believe worship includes choirs and bands, but worship is certainly more than a song, isn't it? The Bible states some strong imperatives when coming before the Lord such as: to clap our hands and shout with joy (Psalm 47:1), to come before His presence with thanksgiving (Psalm 95:2), and to bow down and kneel before the Lord (Psalm 95:6).

These are commands to clap, shout, give thanks, bow down, and kneel. There's nothing about singing a song in those statements. Yet, we're told to sing with joy in Psalm 33:1. In fact, the psalmist goes on to say that we are to sing a "new song" (v. 3). You realize that means singing an inspired or Spirit-led song? Paul called these "supernatural songs" (Ephesians 5:19).

However, worship is so much more than singing, clapping, and shouting. Jesus said, "But an hour is coming, and now is, when true worshipers will worship the Father in spirit and truth; for such people the Father seeks to be His worshipers" (John 4:23). First, Jesus underscored *true* worship, implying that worship can be phony, unspiritual, and even counterfeit. To sing a song about being set free from all chains while still in bondage might be labeled as false declarations. Worship, according to Jesus, must be authentic, real, and rooted in sincerity.

Secondly, Jesus indicated the centrality of all worship: the Father. Worship is always aimed toward Him. In fact, worship is not an initiation on our part, it's actually a response. We are simply responding to His love. God so loved us, the Bible says.

He loved us first, so through worship we are responding to His outrageous love toward us.

Third, Jesus indicated that true worship emanates from the deepest part of our lives. He said we are to worship in "spirit." This surpasses our emotions and feelings. We are never to allow how we feel at the moment to dictate our response to God in worship. My choice to give thanks to God is not only His will for my life, but it often changes the way I feel (1 Thessalonians 5:18). Additionally, true worship is unpretentious because it's wrapped in truth. Therefore, I can be raw and honest before God. His truth actually sets me free (John 8:32).

There's another thought about worship that I want to define, and it's the actual term "worship" (*proskuneo*). This word means to lick the hand like a dog licks the hand of its master. About a year ago, we got a dog—despite our saying that we would never again have a dog. However, my reluctance of owning a pet was quickly overshadowed by the constant affection from this little, twelve-pound miniature dachshund.

The moment that I enter the house, if I allow her, she's in my arms licking my hands, arms, and face. Her constant affection doesn't depend upon what is going on in our world. Politics, finances, sickness, or stresses of ministry are no distraction to this dog. Her affection for me is endless regardless of anything else. Watching her express excitement over my presence might give some idea of this word *proskuneo*.

A Canaanite woman who approached Jesus had no trouble in expressing her affection and love toward Him. Jesus first ignored her, then told her that He wasn't sent for her, and finally said that He wasn't going to offer Israel's bread to her

(Matthew 15:21–28). But nothing stopped her affection for Jesus because she bowed down before Him. The Bible says that she worshiped Him.

This gentile woman was unrestrained and unoffended both by her circumstances and by what Jesus said to her. She knew Jesus was the Son of David—the promised Messiah—who was *the* Lord of all, so she fell at His feet and licked His hand like an affectionate dog. Sounds humiliating, doesn't it? I would like to suggest that humility is the root attitude in true worship. It's the humble, broken, and contrite heart that God will not despise (Psalm 51:17). Those who humble themselves are the ones whom God exalts (James 4:10).

Worship is so much more than a song during a Sunday service. Rather, it's a lifelong attitude of going lower and slower every day. True worship is an increasing affection for God that showers praise and thanksgiving to Him in every moment of our lives regardless of what we walk through. It encompasses every part of your life because you are to live consciously aware of His presence in everything you do.

Therefore, you worship in a variety of ways, such as singing, clapping, dancing, painting, kneeling, praying, working, or simply laying prostrate at His feet in humble adoration. True worship never ends, so we never need to "start" a worship service. In actuality, we only enter into an ongoing celebration that is happening in the heavens.

PRAYER

Dear God, may I live to worship you in everything that I do. Regardless of what I walk through, enable me to give thanks in all things, amen.

APPLICATION

1. Are you a thankful person? Why or why not?
2. What kinds of things enhance your ability to worship God?
3. Read the story about the Canaanite woman in Matthew 15:21-28. What prevented her from being offended with Jesus? Why did Jesus grant her request?
4. Start today by giving thanks to God for all things (1 Thessalonians 5:18).

7

Releasing His Presence

We always release what we're most full of. Crises, challenges, and adversities that we all are confronted with only reveal what we're filled with.

What is released from your life?

I think about that question when I read the story in Acts 3. Peter and John were going to the temple to pray one afternoon. On the way they encountered a man at the gate of the temple who had been crippled for forty years. He sat and begged alms from those entering the temple, and on that occasion he looked to Peter and John for help. "But Peter said, 'I do not possess silver and gold, but what I do have I give to you: In the name of Jesus Christ the Nazarene—walk'" (Acts 3:6).

What did Peter have? The verb "have" (*echo*) means to possess, to hold, or even to wear. One expositor says it means to possess something that possesses you. Peter had the Holy Spirit: He was possessed with the presence of Jesus. In other words, Peter possessed Jesus and Jesus possessed Peter, so when a crisis confronted the apostle, he gave away what he had.

It once was stated, "The Church is no longer able to say to the lame, 'rise and walk' because of the fact that the Church can no longer say, 'silver and gold have I none.'" In his book, *Whatever Happened to Worship?*, A. W. Tozer linked churches and Christians today with the believers in Laodicea who thought that they were rich and wealthy and in need of nothing. Yet, in reality, they were "wretched and miserable and poor and blind and naked" (Revelation 3:17b).

I hope that isn't true of your life or your church. Without the power and presence of the Holy Spirit in our lives, we really have nothing of value to give away. I'm not against having riches and resources, but the greatest blessing that we can release is the presence of Jesus — if in fact, that's who we're filled with.

We always release what we're most full of. I'm challenged by the story that Dennis Kinlaw once told. The one-time president of Asbury College referenced a speaker who stood before the student body with a glass of water in his hand, and the speaker asked someone to come forward and shake his arm. Of course, when the speaker's arm was shaken, water spilled all over the floor. The speaker asked: "So why did water spill?" Everyone answered the obvious by stating that the speaker's arm had been shaken.

He asked the question again with a bit of emphasis: "Why did *water* spill?" People caught on and then answered: "Because water was in the glass." Kinlaw went on to explain that what spilled out of the glass was not determined by the shaking, but what spilled out was determined by what filled the glass. If the speaker held a glass of milk, then milk would have spilled on the floor. If juice was in the glass, then juice is what would have spilled on the floor.

Crises, challenges, and adversities that we all are confronted with only reveal what we're filled with. It's the reason, Kinlaw stressed, that every Christian must be completely filled with and walking in the power of the Holy Spirit. Jesus said, "He who believes in Me, as the Scripture said, 'From his innermost being will flow rivers of living water'" (John 7:38). This living water represents the Holy Spirit, and it should flow out of us and touch people around us. When Peter faced a troubling situation, he released the presence of Jesus—the one thing that he was filled with. Immediately the crippled man's feet and ankles were strengthened, and he leaped in the air, walked, and praised God.

I have no problems giving away material resources when necessary. This Scripture in Acts 3:6 isn't stating a mandate against giving money to those in need, but what a tragedy if we *only* have silver and gold to give away. The greatest impartation that we can give someone is the presence of Jesus. We don't need to be in a crisis, either, to give away Jesus. Every moment of our day becomes an opportunity to release His presence. The adventure never has to end. When you go to a restaurant, go there to give away Jesus. Eating a meal should be secondary. When you go to the store, go there to release His presence. Purchasing eggs and milk should become a second thought.

I remember standing at the checkout counter one time and looking into the eyes of the young lady behind the counter. She had a nametag that said, "Rita." The Holy Spirit spoke to me about some of the problems she was facing with her family. I mentioned something about that to her and asked if I could pray. With tears running down her face, my wife and I gave Jesus away to her. It took no more than forty-five seconds.

Another time my friend and I prayed with a waiter to receive Christ. A woman in our church prayed for someone with back issues, and God instantly healed the person. Story after story and life after life, it's simply releasing the presence of the Holy Spirit upon people wherever we might find ourselves. I believe that the moment you walk into a room the atmosphere can shift if you carry His presence within you.

We carry within us the supernatural power of the Holy Spirit (John 14:17 and Acts 1:8). Think about that: you and I can give away the most life-changing force. The next time you are standing face-to-face with someone, think about the blessing that you can release. And should you be in a difficult situation that shakes you, release the same Holy Spirit. If you are filled with the Holy Spirit, never hang your head over what you *don't* have. Live with the confidence that you can release the presence of Jesus to the needy world around you.

PRAYER

Jesus, fill me with your Holy Spirit to the point that I overflow. The next time I'm standing in front of someone, let me release your presence all over them, amen.

APPLICATION

1. What kinds of things come out of your mouth when you are agitated?
2. Can you describe a time when you released the presence of Jesus to someone?
3. Do you believe that you are possessed with the Holy Spirit? If you're not sure, take a moment to ask the Holy Spirit to fill you.

8

Perseverance

Victory is always found on the other side of the greatest challenges if we'll simply persevere and never quit.

Recently, I heard a challenging message by an international speaker named Christine Caine. In her hands she held an old roll of film, and she explained how it had to be developed in a dark room before the images could be seen. The development process takes time and patience. The film must remain in the dark for a specific period of time before it can be brought into the light. If it is exposed to the light too soon, the images are ruined. Caine explained how often we enter a season of waiting and it seems dark and lonely. Yet, if we're steadfast through that period of time, it can enhance the image of Christ in our lives. The message was a call to perseverance.

There are eight major values that our church embraces. To us, they are pillars to sustaining a revival culture. Of the eight, the one that challenges me the most is "perseverance." Regardless of what you list as values in your life and ministry, this much is for sure: you will have to persevere if you ever hope to accomplish anything significant for the kingdom of God.

I believe that perseverance is the most challenging value because in our American culture we loathe waiting. We have everything from express mail to microwave ovens and fast food to overnight shipping. We are impetuous people who desire instant results, and we don't like having to endure trials, hardships, and difficulties. Most of us detest the idea of persevering. Yet, everything I read in the Bible indicates that those who finished well were those who endured the most, and they persevered until they experienced the breakthrough that they believed was possible.

Paul entered the city of Ephesus for the first time and found twelve guys who had been baptized under John's ministry. After explaining Jesus Christ to them, they were baptized in His name and received the Holy Spirit. Being forced out of teaching in the synagogue by hardened and disobedient people, Paul began reasoning *daily* in the school of Tyrannus, and he did the same regiment for two years. He never stopped preaching the Word. He never quit or shrank back. One scholar indicated that Paul taught the Word for more than 3,000 hours over a period of two years. He kept sowing into the Spirit until breakthrough was experienced (Galatians 6:8–9).

Eventually, a mighty revival broke out in the city of Ephesus, and people began confessing their sins and turning to Christ. They burned their cultic books and ceased practicing magic. The Bible says, "So the word of the Lord was growing mightily and prevailing" (Acts 19:20). The Word of God became so widely known that everyone who lived in

Asia heard it (Acts 19:10). That is a remarkable report, but it occurred because one man refused to quit. Paul persevered until the kingdom of God came to Ephesus and made a transformational difference.

What about your city? I've pastored in Columbus, Ohio, since 1997, and we still have so much work to do. Our city hasn't experienced a major breakthrough yet, but we continue sowing the Word. We're making inroads into the community one life at a time. We're praying for people to be born again, we're crying out for bodies to be healed, we're seeking God for marriages and families to be restored, and we're pressing into His presence, believing for a mighty outpouring of God's Holy Spirit on our church and every church in our city.

We must persevere through trials and adversities, though. We have to believe Isaiah when he declared that we will pass *through* the waters and fire without being harmed (Isaiah 43:2). Victory is always found on the other side of the greatest challenges if we'll simply persevere and never quit.

The early church in the book of Acts was known for its perseverance. Read the accounts of these early believers. They didn't cease proclaiming the Word no matter what happened to them. When threatened because of their boldness, they cried out for even *more* boldness (Acts 4:29-31). When told to be silent about the faith, they refused to listen to any other voice but God's voice (Acts 5:29). When they were persecuted and flogged for their faith, they celebrated that they were worthy enough to suffer for God (Acts 5:41). And in the end, most of them were martyred for choosing Jesus over the world because they knew it was the only way to bring Jesus *to* the world.

What's our excuse? What's our reason for quitting? What prevents us from persevering? Is it because people are leaving our churches? Is it because the pastor preaches too long? Is it because the music is too loud? Is it because we got fired from our job? Is it because our prayer hasn't been answered yet? Is it because people are criticizing us? What keeps us from persevering until the breakthrough is realized in our lives? The early believers were unceasing and relentless in their pursuit of God and in their mission to bring the kingdom to the entire world. They persevered, and because they did, the church of Jesus Christ prevailed.

My challenge to you is to determine this minute that you will not shrink back no matter what (Hebrews 10:38). Don't give up in your season of waiting no matter how dark and difficult your journey seems. Keep pressing into the manifest presence of Jesus—even if you're surrounded by sleepy-eyed, passionless people.

Keep believing God for signs, miracles, and wonders—even if you are criticized and called a proponent of "strange fire." Keep praying for healing, even though people are still sick and diseased, because the Word still says the prayer of faith will save the sick (James 5:15). Believe God for that revival, trust Him for those marriages, continue to cry out for those prodigals, and remain faithful to your calling no matter what.

Persevere to the end, my friends, and keep on sowing to the Spirit. Your *harvest* is upon you.

PRAYER

Father, I choose today to persevere until the breakthrough occurs. Empower me to never shrink back no matter what, amen.

APPLICATION

1. What are some of the obstacles that you are up against right now?
2. Is it difficult for you to persevere, or are you committed to your task?
3. What steps can you take to remain faithful to what you've been called to do?
4. Who are some of the most courageous—nonquitters—that you know? If possible, have them commit to pray for you.

9

Never Quit

Some of you may be one prayer away from the greatest victory in your life, so don't quit.

As I travel across the nation and look into the eyes of God's people, there seems to be a universal challenge facing Christ followers, and it is the challenge of overcoming discouragement. Discouragement is a real battle for God's people. Some are fighting financial battles while others are walking through physical issues. Still others are facing spiritual or emotional struggles, and some people are facing extreme persecution.

No one is exempt from battles this side of eternity. Jesus clearly told us that in this world we would experience tribulation (John 16:33), and add to this the reality that we face a real enemy whose occupation is to steal, kill, and destroy (John 10:10).

Satan desires to play "mind games" with Christ followers, which is the actual meaning of "schemes", found in 2 Corinthians 2:11. The apostle Paul went on to write, "But I am afraid that, as the serpent deceived Eve by his craftiness, your minds will be led astray from the simplicity and purity *of devotion* to Christ" (2 Corinthians 11:3). The enemy will plant thoughts in our minds, such as your prayers will never make a difference, this situation will never change, that person will never seek the Lord, you will never be healed, or your church will never be revived. On and on it goes, the mind games continue with the purpose of causing discouragement so that we'll drop out of the spiritual race.

Jesus told a parable about ceaseless prayer so that we would not lose heart but continue to pray day and night until God brings the breakthrough (Luke 18:1-7). In another parable, Jesus insisted that we continue to ask, seek, and knock with persistence (shameless audacity) until the Holy Spirit is poured out on the situation (Luke 11:5-13). The point is Jesus recognized the challenge we would face concerning discouragement, but blessing always comes to those who refuse to quit pressing into Him.

I wish that I could tell you when your prodigals will be redeemed, when your church will turn around, or when your disease will be healed. I may not know the actual day of your breakthrough, but I know Jesus said, "If you ask Me anything in My name, I will do it" (John 14:14). I believe Jesus is a promise keeper, don't you? Jesus said elsewhere, "Truly, truly, I say to you, if you ask the Father for anything in My name, He will give it to you" (John 16:23b). I realize that these promises aren't guarantees for our self-centered whims, but if we've died to ourselves and live for Jesus alone, then His desires spur on our tenacious prayers.

I love the promise the apostle Paul gave us: he wrote, "Let us not lose heart in doing good, for in due time we will reap if we do not grow weary" (Galatians 6:9). To lose heart (*enkakeo*) means to become so discouraged or disheartened that all enthusiasm to continue ceases. So, we cease praying, fasting, worshiping, and believing. We cease praying with expectancy and stop celebrating with victory. We then align ourselves to earthly realities rather than heavenly possibilities.

But Paul is stating the mandate to not quit, to not stop, and to not throw in the towel. Listen again to the promise that he wrote: in due time, in the right moment, and in the correct season "we *will* reap" the blessing. Paul didn't say "maybe" or "possibly." He said that "we will reap" if we continue sowing to the Spirit.

Sowing and reaping is something that I've been a part of for nearly sixteen years. We have a very large garden in our yard, and each year I sow seeds into the soil. I've never planted seeds and picked the harvest the same day. Gardening is a matter of perseverance: it takes time and endurance. Some vegetables don't produce a harvest until sixty days after they've been sown, but it doesn't stop me from sowing year after year. Harvest time is always a blessing for the McCorkle family and has been for many years. How much more should we anticipate the spiritual harvest if we continue to sow to the Spirit!

What if we continue sowing to the Spirit for revival in our church, city, and nation? What if we continue believing and praying for healing, restoration, deliverance, and for His kingdom to come? Paul wasn't discouraged by the hard-hearted people in Ephesus who made it difficult for him to preach. He refused to quit sowing the Word for two years and eventually everyone in Asia heard the truth (Acts 19:10). Unusual miracles broke out, people confessed their sins, and a church was birthed because one man continued to sow into the Spirit. Maybe this is why Paul wrote, "Therefore, my beloved brethren, be steadfast, immovable, always abounding in the work of the Lord, knowing that your toil is not *in* vain in the Lord" (1 Corinthians 15:58).

My dear brothers and sisters, I have no idea what some of you are walking through. But I know who functions through you. You are possessed by the living God. You are filled with the extraordinary power of the Holy Spirit; therefore, "[You] can do all things through Him who strengthens [you]" (Philippians 4:13). Jesus said, "All things are possible to him who believes" (Mark 9:23b). I believe "all things" means just that: all things!

Whatever you're facing, whatever is challenging you, or whatever might be standing in front of you, refuse to quit. Refuse to shrink back (Hebrews 10:38). Don't align yourself to the lies of the enemy—he's a loser.

Some of you may be one prayer away from the greatest victory in your life, so don't quit.

PRAYER

God, I pray for a spirit of perseverance to fill our hearts. Give courage, hope, and strength to all of us as we continue to sow to the Spirit, in Jesus' name, amen.

APPLICATION

1. Are there some things in your life that are tempting you to be discouraged?
2. Can you identify some of the mind games that the enemy is playing on you?
3. What are some promises that you are holding out for?
4. Hold to the Word that says "you will reap if we do not grow weary" in Galatians 6:9. Don't quit sowing to the Spirit in all that you do.

10
Lower and Slower

Going slower actually means becoming a better listener than a talker, and it means becoming a better leader for Jesus by being a better follower of Him.

In 2013, I had the privilege of completing a doctor of ministry degree with a group of eighteen amazing people from around the world. One of those persons in my group was Rolland Baker. Together with his wife, Heidi, they minister to the impoverished and downtrodden of Mozambique.

Their stories are incredible, and for hours our group would hear testimonies of God's amazing love being poured out. The number of people coming to Christ is almost staggering, not to mention the extraordinary miracles of healing and even dead bodies being raised to life. My faith soared as we heard testimonies of God's power and love bringing redemption, restoration, and hope to needy people. But there was one message shared by Rolland and Heidi that challenged me more than any other, and that was the message of going lower and slower.

Those two words run contrary to our culture, and they even pose a problem for the contemporary church. Let's unfold these words so that we can come to a better understanding of what it means to move lower and slower. First, to go lower means to choose a path of humility. Jesus said, "Whoever exalts himself shall be humbled; and whoever humbles himself shall be exalted" (Matthew 23:12).

This statement by Jesus contains both active and passive verbs. An active verb is something that we choose to do while a passive verb is something that inevitably happens to us. Therefore, if we choose to "exalt" ourselves, there will eventually be a time when we are "humbled." Conversely, if we choose to "humble" ourselves, we will be "exalted." I hope that we will choose to humble ourselves before the Lord as a way of life (James 4:10). The apostle Paul told us to possess the same attitude as Jesus had, which was a life of downward mobility (Philippians 2:5-8).

Everywhere I look, however, I see the push for upward mobility. People are striving for the next perk or promotion, the next big break, or the next great opportunity. I'm reminded of the disciples who came to Jesus and said, "Teacher, we want You to do for us whatever we ask of You" (Mark 10:35b). Their audacity was only surpassed by what they actually wanted: the top spot in the kingdom of heaven with Jesus. Jesus cut through their ambitions with the call to become a servant. Truly, to be great is to be a servant of all.

Humility looks for opportunities to quietly serve others and to do so without the need for recognition.

What *does* it mean to be humble? Humility is from a Latin derivative that means ground, humus, or dirt. Nothing is lower than dirt. Yet, good soil (humble dirt), Jesus said, has the capacity to "bear fruit thirty, sixty, and a hundredfold" (Mark 4:20b).

Keep in mind that humility is not self-condemnation or self-denunciation. When someone pays you a compliment, simply respond with a kind "thank you." Too often we think being humble is to loathe a compliment by stating how terrible we are. Brigid Hermon wrote in the early 1900s that most of what we call humility, especially the habit of self-accusation and self-abatement, is actually the fruit of self-obsession and, in reality, is nothing more than a deep sense of sin and pride.[4]

To be humble is to remain teachable, too. In fact, we should be able to learn from anyone no matter his or her pedigree or education. Additionally, humble people function well under authority because they are not rebellious. They honor those above them, and they have a unique ability to inconspicuously encourage others around them. Everyone around a humble person is elevated and treated with respect and even a sense of reverence. I want to go lower, don't you?

Second, going slower means becoming love. The greater our influence becomes, the slower our walk should be. We must learn to take time for people around us and to actually look them in the eyes and pay attention to their needs. I believe when Jesus looked at people, He looked "into" them and saw their hearts. The most important person in the world is the person in front of you at that moment. Don't walk up to a counter while on the phone or plop down in a bus or plane seat wearing headphones. If you do, you've just communicated to people around you that they are unimportant. Several times in the New Testament Jesus "stopped" for people. Usually, it was someone whom society had moved away from. Jesus moved slowly through the crowds, and He took time to minister to their needs.

I'm challenged by the first characteristic of love listed by Paul in 1 Corinthians 13:4. He wrote, "Love is patient...." To be patient (*makrothumeo*) means to continually wait on other people without losing heart. Too many times I've grown impatient with someone, hoping that they would change in "my time." Time is relative to God. That's why I'm told to cry out day and night so that He can move "quickly" in my life (Luke 18:7-8). God will move quickly if I move slower—by that I mean moving in rhythm with the Holy Spirit.

I'm on a quest to move in step with the Spirit and that usually means slowing my life down enough to hear His voice. Going slower actually means becoming a better listener than a talker, and it means becoming a better leader for Jesus by being a better follower of Him. My life is being adjusted by this simple phrase of going lower and slower. What about you?

PRAYER

Jesus, will you empower me to walk lower and slower. As I read about your life in the Scriptures, this was your lifestyle. I choose to follow your example, amen.

APPLICATION

1. Can you identify people in your life who demonstrate a lifestyle of lower and slower?
2. Do you believe that your life is characterized by humility?
3. Do you believe that your life is characterized by love?
4. Spend some time in reading the gospels. As you observe Jesus' life, realize that you have the same Holy Spirit in you that Jesus had in Him. The Spirit will enable you to become lower and slower.

11

Sustaining The Fire

Fruit bearing never has to end. We are to be spiritually healthy and vibrant all of our lives.

Are you more passionate for Jesus today than you were six months ago?

One of the most discouraging observations I've discovered is to find people who over time have lost their passion for Jesus. When they first came to Christ, people would describe them as being on fire, but time and circumstances seemed to have squelched their flames.

The Bible, however, paints a picture of sustainability. Psalm 1:2 speaks of someone who delights in the law of God. Literally, they take pleasure in the Word of the Lord to the point that they meditate on it day and night. The result is, "He will be like a tree *firmly* planted by streams of water, Which yields its fruit in its season And its leaf does not wither; And in whatever he does, he prospers" (Psalm 1:3).

Note the Psalmist said, "And its leaf does not wither." How many believers over the course of time spiritually wither? Another passage says, "The righteous man will flourish like the palm tree, He will grow like a cedar in Lebanon. Planted in the house of the LORD, They will flourish in the courts of our God. They will still yield fruit in old age; They shall be full of sap and very green" (Psalm 92:12-14). Fruit bearing never has to end according to this passage. We are to be spiritually healthy and vibrant all of our lives.

Still, another passage says, "Blessed is the man who trusts in the LORD And whose trust is the LORD. For he will be like a tree planted by the water, That extends its roots by the stream And will not fear when the heat comes; But its leaves will be green, And it will not be anxious in a year of drought Nor cease to yield fruit" (Jeremiah 17:7-8). This passage describes a person who never stops producing fruit. They are always green, which is a metaphor for being spiritually healthy.

In fact, the person described in Jeremiah is so spiritually healthy that adversity doesn't produce fear or anxiety. These passages are setting the standard for spiritual sustainability. There are too many Christians who are characteristically unstable, marked by zeal one day but later they fizzle out.

The passage that really inspires me is Romans 12:9-13. It says, "*Let* love *be* without hypocrisy. Abhor what is evil; cling to what is good. *Be* devoted to one another in brotherly love; give preference to one another in honor; not lagging behind in diligence, fervent in spirit, serving the Lord; rejoicing in hope, persevering in tribulation, devoted to prayer, contributing to the needs of the saints, practicing hospitality."

I want to underscore this phrase: "Not lagging behind in diligence, fervent in spirit." The NIV Bible says, "Never lacking in zeal, but keep your spiritual fervor." The AMP Bible says, "Never lag in zeal and in earnest endeavor; but aglow and burning with the Spirit." Fervent (*zeo*) is defined as cooking, burning, boiling; on fire or always hot. This present tense verb describes a believer who is always spiritually hot and full of enthusiasm. As Christians we are to always be on fire! Little wonder, then, that the Lord will spit "lukewarm" believers from His mouth (Revelation 3:16).

Being on fire is much more than merely being emotionally charged. It has everything to do with your intensity and devotion for Christ. When you're on fire, your greatest love, your deepest passion, and your highest affection is Jesus and His manifest presence. Worship is not a mundane, apathetic event, but rather you live to worship the Lord. The Word is consumed with an insatiable desire, and the love of God spills lavishly from your life.

If you're going to remain on fire for God, keep three things in mind. First, staying on fire has little to do with how you feel. "But My righteous one shall live by faith . . ." (Hebrews 10:38a), not by feelings. Don't ride the waves of your emotions: they are great followers but terrible leaders. Staying on fire is a choice of your will, not your emotions.

Second, staying on fire has little to do with others. Your relationship with God cannot be contingent upon others; otherwise, you will become dependent upon people to sustain your spiritual vibrancy and not on the Holy Spirit. You have to cultivate your passion in the secret place with God, and you must discover Him for yourself in the chamber room.

I'm not advocating Christian isolation. But, while people can encourage you and spur you on, intimacy with Jesus is forged when you decide that Christ and Christ alone is all you need. King David's men spoke of stoning him because they were so embittered, ". . . But David "strengthened himself in the Lord his God" (1 Samuel 30:6b). People will often fail you and sometimes hurt you, but you've been given the Holy Spirit who will strengthen you.

Third, staying on fire has little to do with results. If you measure your spiritual vibrancy by results, you will be quickly misled. Miracles, manifestations, success, failure, great gain, or great loss should not hinder or enhance your fire for God. Keep your eyes on Jesus and not results. I've left meetings where almost everyone in the room was touched and healed, and I've left other services where it seemed as if very few people were touched. Leave the results to Jesus — just keep pressing into Him.

My prayer for you and me is that we will cultivate spiritual sustainability in our lives. I'm praying that we will always stay on fire for God.

PRAYER

God, fill me afresh with your Holy Spirit. Fan the flames of my heart and stir up my passion for you, Jesus, in your name, amen.

APPLICATION

1. What are some ways that you can increase your fervor and affection for Jesus Christ?
2. Can you identify people in your life who are spiritual on fire? What makes them that way?
3. Review the three factors pointed out in this lesson: 1) Staying on fire has little to do with how you feel. 2) Staying on fire has little to do with others. 3) Staying on fire has little to do with results. Realize that you can grow in your spiritual passion for Christ.

12

Don't Be Led Astray

There are too many Christians who have Jesus in their hearts, but the enemy is in their heads.

The apostle Paul admitted to being afraid of something. Of course, everything that I've read about him in the Bible would indicate that he was fearless. For example, when Paul was preaching the gospel in a city called Lystra, Jews came from the surrounding areas of Antioch and Iconium, and after they stirred up the crowds, they stoned him. Supposing Paul to be dead, they dragged his body out of the city and left him. The Bible says, "But while the disciples stood around him, he got up and entered the city" (Acts 14:20a).

It might be worth mentioning that when Paul "got up," it also means to be raised up from the dead. Some scholars believe that Paul *was* dead and that the disciples raised him to life. Whether he was dead or not makes no difference to the point that I want to underscore. What really challenges me about Paul is that when he got up he went back into the city where he was persecuted. Not only that, he actually returned to the two cities where the angry Jews came from: Antioch and Iconium.

While most people would have packed their bags and left town, Paul returned to the very place where he was stoned to death. How is that for fearlessness? It's this guy who wrote, "But I am afraid that, as the serpent deceived Eve by his craftiness, . . ." (2 Corinthians 11:3a). Granted, by his own admission he was speaking with a bit of hyperbole and foolishness when he said that, but the truth remains that there was something substantial that weighed heavily on Paul's heart.

Paul began by stating, "For I am jealous for you with a godly jealousy; for I betrothed you to one husband, so that to Christ I might present you as a pure virgin" (2 Corinthians 11:2). That had profound meaning in that culture because when a woman was betrothed to a man there were enormous consequences if a woman defiled her body with someone else prior to the wedding. Sometimes a couple could be betrothed for months before the wedding, but the couple was legally bound to each other. Paul stated that we have been betrothed to one husband—Jesus Christ. Our loyalty is to Jesus and Him alone. We are to have no other "love affair" above Jesus.

One day we will be consummated with Christ. This will be a grand and glorious day when we are presented to Christ, our Bridegroom, and we will spend all eternity together. However, until Jesus comes to receive us unto Himself, we are to remain faithful to Him alone. There will be serious consequences if we defile our hearts by putting other lovers before Jesus. Do you still love Him? Is Jesus your *first* love?

Don't Be Led Astray

My prayer is that we will be the faithful bride who can be presented before Christ, ". . . having no spot or wrinkle or any such thing; but that she would be holy and blameless" (Ephesians 5:27b).

Paul's desire to present a chaste virgin to the Lord continued in the next verse when he stated his fear. He said, "But I am afraid that, as the serpent deceived Eve by his craftiness, your minds will be led astray from the simplicity and purity *of devotion* to Christ" (2 Corinthians 11:3). If there was one fear that seized Paul, it was this: he didn't want the enemy to get into the minds of believers and lead them astray.

I can tell you that this is what weighs heavily on my heart as a senior leader of a church. I'm so blessed when people come to faith and stand to share their testimonies. I can't begin to describe the joy that I have when people experience breakthrough and devote their lives to God. There is no greater pleasure than to watch people fall in love with Jesus, worship with passion, and pray with fervor. Yet, I carry a burden, perhaps even a fear like Paul did, that the enemy will cause people to be led astray by getting into their minds. What was the enemy's tactics with Eve?

First, the serpent wanted Eve to question God's goodness. The implication behind his question about not being able to eat from every tree was that God wasn't entirely good (Genesis 3:1). If you question God's goodness, then you won't trust Him when difficult times come. The enemy will say things like, "Maybe you're sick because God is angry with you," or "Why did God let that happen to you?" Here's a big one: "If you really mattered to God, you wouldn't have to walk through this." These are things Satan says to make us question God's goodness.

Second, the serpent wanted Eve to doubt God's Word. The question the serpent posed led Eve to doubt the validity of what God declared. Only God's Word is truth (John 17:17). If we question the Word, then we will put greater faith in our circumstances than in what He said. We'll become sabotaged by oppressive fear and anxiety. Like Peter, we will sink because the wind and waves will appear greater than Jesus (Matthew 14:30).

Paul said one time that he wasn't ignorant of Satan's "schemes" (2 Corinthians 2:11). This word schemes (*noema*) can be translated as "mind games." Satan loves to play mind games with God's people. There are too many Christians who have Jesus in their hearts, but the enemy is in their heads. If we let our minds become infected with Satan's tricks, then we'll be led astray from the simplicity and purity to Christ.

Set your minds on things above (Colossians 3:2). Keep your eyes focused on Jesus and Him alone (Hebrews 12:2). Live by faith and not by sight (2 Corinthians 4:18). Additionally, combat the lies of the enemy with the truth of God's Word. Saturate your mind with the Scriptures. Read the Bible until it reads you. If you will immerse yourself in the Word, then you'll recognize falsehoods quicker. Let's remain faithful to Jesus so that we can be presented to Him as pure virgins.

PRAYER

Lord God, I choose today to trust your Word. Empower me to walk consistently with you no matter what, amen.

APPLICATION

1. Has the enemy ever tried to make you question God's Word? If so, how?
2. Have you ever questioned God's goodness? Why or why not?
3. Identify several passages of Scripture that keep you anchored when you are being challenged.

13

Greater Than You Think

If we're not careful, we will spurn the seemingly small and insignificant opportunities requested of us by Jesus. Yet our faithfulness to obey His voice regardless of surface evidence can produce a harvest of many souls for the kingdom.

I can't begin to count the times I've believed that what I did for Christ seemed totally insignificant. Jesus has been teaching me to keep my eyes solely on Him and to simply accomplish what He asks of me without measuring the results. There's a passage in Mark that illustrates this subject matter. It begins this way: "On that day, when evening came, He said to them, 'Let us go over to the other side.' Leaving the crowd, they took Him along with them in the boat, just as He was; and other boats were with Him" (Mark 4:35-36).

Note the phrase "on that day." That very day Jesus had taught the crowds about sowing and reaping. In Mark 4:3-20, Jesus spoke about the sower scattering seed and about how some soil (people) could hear the Word and produce fruit thirty, sixty, and a hundredfold. In Mark 4:26-29, He spoke about how quickly the seed could produce a harvest, and in Mark 4:30-32, He taught about how the smallest seed could produce the greatest harvest.

At the end of *that day* Jesus essentially said, "Let's put this teaching into practice on the other side of the lake." So, the disciples left the crowd—which many of us will need to do from time to time if we're going to obey Jesus—and they sailed for the other side.

What was on the other side? Initially, it didn't look like a large harvest. On the other side of the sea, Jesus was met by a demonized man who lived among tombs. He was unable to be bound by shackles and chains. He lived a tormented life screaming night and day while he gashed himself with stones. When Jesus stepped on the scene, this demonically tormented man fell before Him and said, "My name is Legion; for we are many" (Mark 5:9b). Legion is a Latin term meaning a Roman regiment, and it refers to a number equivalent to over 6,000.

The point is this man was being vexed by many demons, and they didn't want to leave that region (Mark 5:10). Jesus was just north of Decapolis, an area that was deeply infested with sin, humanism, immorality, and various religions. It was probably no different from your city or mine. Demonic powers and principalities often find their resting place over territories where churches pose little threat to their operations.

All of that was about to change because Jesus permitted over 6,000 demons to fill a herd of swine. However, the pigs couldn't tolerate what people often do, and they rushed off a steep bank and about 2,000 of them drowned. The herdsmen reported the incident to people in the city, and when they came to inspect the damage, they implored, begged, and pleaded with Jesus to leave their region in spite of the fact that this previously demonized man was now clothed and in his right mind.

As Jesus was getting into the boat to leave that region, the man who had been delivered requested to accompany Him. Jesus, however, told him to go back into Decapolis and tell of the great things that Jesus had done (Mark 5:19). On the surface, that day looked like a giant failure. Outside of one person being delivered, no one else that day was open to the seeds that were being sown. Jesus had asked His disciples to go to the other side to sow seed and for what? They were kicked out of the city. The crusade got shut down, and they were told to leave.

At first glance, we might have the tendency to complain about such a small harvest, but here is the rest of the story. Mark 5:20 indicates that this transformed man began to proclaim the great things that Jesus did, and those who heard his testimony were amazed. When Jesus came back a second time to Decapolis months later, the people didn't request that Jesus leave their region—not this time. Instead, they brought to Him someone who needed to be healed, and they implored Jesus to lay hands on him (Mark 7:31-32).

Additionally, crowds gathered for several days, and Jesus, who was moved with compassion, multiplied seven loaves and some fish. About 4,000 people were ministered to in the very region that Jesus was once asked to leave (Mark 8:1-9).

I find it interesting that the first time Jesus was near Decapolis He sowed a small mustard seed—much like the story that He told before sailing to the other side (Mark 4:30-32). If we're not careful, we will spurn the seemingly small and insignificant opportunities requested of us by Jesus. Yet our faithfulness to obey His voice—regardless of surface evidence—can produce a harvest of many souls for the kingdom. Don't ever judge the size of your harvest by the size of what you've sown, and don't minimize the transformation of only a few people. It only takes one person who has been significantly touched by God's mercy to affect an entire city.

Years ago, A. W. Tozer warned the church of the dangers of statistics, numbers, and law of averages. He cautioned against the ecclesiastical structures that kept Christians focused on such "unspiritual" things. When we operate from the realm of the kingdom of God, we discover that little is much in the hands of God.

From a kingdom perspective, we learn that God takes the foolish things, the weak things, and the despised things, and He accomplishes amazing results. From His viewpoint, there are not wasted efforts if we're completely obedient to His assignments. So, keep on sowing to the Spirit, and you will reap a harvest if you don't give up (Galatians 6:8-9).

PRAYER

Jesus, forgive me for being more concerned with results than with obedience. Help me to follow You wherever You lead and sow seeds into everyone I meet. And may the harvest be greater than I could ever imagine, in Jesus' name, amen.

APPLICATION

1. Where is the Lord asking you to sow spiritual seeds?
2. Have you ever been discouraged by what looked like little results after doing what the Lord asked of you?
3. How do you handle seemingly small results?
4. Begin to ask the Lord to use you *His* way without criticizing the task or results.

14

Doing What Jesus Did

Being like Jesus must include preaching, teaching, healing, seeking and saving the lost, and destroying the works of the devil. We must give ourselves to supernatural, miraculous activities if we are to be like Jesus.

Most of us would agree that the essence of holiness is Christlikeness, right? At the end of the day, if our lives don't exemplify Jesus, then I would suggest that we're chasing the wrong things. Jesus should be the centrality of our churches, ministries, and lives. John said, "The one who says he abides in Him ought himself to walk in the same manner as He walked" (1 John 2:6). What does it mean to walk as Jesus did? Stated differently, how do we discover His central mission?

My friend and scholar Jon Ruthven asked four questions to discover what Jesus did and what we're supposed to look like as New Testament believers. First, what is it that the New Testament says Jesus came to do? The Bible summarizes

Jesus' ministry by the following: preaching, teaching, healing, seeking and saving the lost, and destroying the works of the devil (Matthew 4:23 and 9:35; Luke 19:10; 1 John 3:8).

Second, what did He actually spend His time doing? The answer would be preaching, teaching, healing, seeking and saving the lost, and destroying the works of the devil. Third, what did Jesus tell His disciples to do? Well, He told them to do the same as He did: preach, teach, heal, seek and save the lost, and destroy the works of the devil (Matthew 10:1-8; Luke 10:9; 10:19).

Fourth, what is it that they actually spent their time doing? They spent their time preaching, teaching, healing, seeking and saving the lost, and destroying the works of the devil. Obviously, the next question is: what should we be spending our time doing? I propose to you that if our central activities as followers of Jesus aren't preaching, teaching, healing, seeking and saving the lost, and destroying the works of the devil, then we've drifted from the main emphasis of New Testament Christianity.

As Jesus was nearing the end of His days on earth, He pulled back the curtains to His heart by sharing with His disciples some essential instructions. During His final hours He said, "Truly, truly, I say to you, he who believes in Me, the works that I do, he will do also; and greater *works* than these he will do; because I go to the Father" (John 14:12). Works (*ergon*) mean deeds, activities, accomplishments, and efforts.

If we note the space devoted to the works of Jesus in terms of miraculous deeds and supernatural activities that is recorded in the gospels, the percentages are very revealing.

Supernatural, miraculous works comprise 44 percent of Matthew, 65 percent of Mark, 29 percent of Luke, and 30 percent of John.

Additionally, when you examine the believers in the book of Acts, 49.7 percent of their works were given to supernatural, miraculous activities, such as healing, prophecies, and spiritual transformation of people and cities. These percentages should tell us that Jesus not only gave Himself to this kind of ministry, but He commissioned and empowered His followers to exemplify Him—and, in fact, they did.

When Jesus deployed His disciples, He said, "And as you go, preach, saying 'The kingdom of heaven is at hand.' Heal *the* sick, raise *the* dead, cleanse *the* lepers, cast out demons. Freely you received, freely give'" (Matthew 10:7-8). When He deployed seventy others, He sent them in pairs to heal the sick and tell them that the kingdom of God had come near (Luke 10:9). My point is that being like Jesus *must* include preaching, teaching, healing, seeking and saving the lost, and destroying the works of the devil. We must give ourselves to supernatural, miraculous activities if we are to be like Jesus.

Not long ago I was talking with someone who had graduated from a Bible college, and their degree was in religion. They were eager to enter the ministry, so I proceeded to ask them how many classes they had concerning the supernatural activities of Jesus. I wanted to know if they learned how to heal the sick, cast out demons, or destroy the works of the devil through Spirit-led prayer. They laughed aloud when I asked them because they didn't have one class that emphasized the very activities that Jesus spent His time doing and then deployed His followers to do.

What is even worse is that the miraculous, supernatural works that Jesus did and commissioned us to do were spurned and depreciated during their educational process. Are we in trouble? Something is wrong in our educational and discipleship process if we're not emphasizing the works that Jesus did. I'm not downplaying being like Jesus in terms of oneness with the Father (John 17:21), walking in love and humility (John 13:14–15), or living with moral integrity (John 8:46). I'm merely underscoring the fact that if we're going to be like Jesus, then we should be like Him in regard to the extraordinary works that He did, too.

The truth is you've been "clothed with power from on high" (Luke 24:49b). You are filled with God's Holy Spirit! Think about that for a moment, the One who preached, healed, cast out demons, and raised the dead lives inside you. This is the mystery that was hidden for ages, "Christ in you, the hope of glory" (Colossians 1:27b). It's time to let Him out. "Now to Him who is able to do far more abundantly beyond all that we ask or think, according to the power that works within us" (Ephesians 3:20). Take the risk, release His presence, and be amazed by how Jesus uses you. It's time to be just like Him.

PRAYER

Dear God, you've empowered me to replicate Jesus. Use me to preach, teach, heal, seek and save the lost, and destroy the works of the devil. I want to do what you did, Jesus, all the days of my life. In your name I pray, amen.

APPLICATION

1. What kinds of things come to your mind when you think about being like Jesus?
2. Do you believe that you are more like Jesus today than you were a year ago? Why or why not?
3. What kinds of things keep you from Christlikeness? What kinds of things enable you to be more like Him?

15

The One Thing

If you haven't found the one thing in your life, you will be distracted by the "many things," and most of them will lead you away from Jesus.

What is the "one thing" that you will do in your life?

We are a busy people, no doubt. We're able to accomplish more things in one day than our grandparents did in one month. Modern conveniences promise to save time when, in reality, they have increased activities. So, to narrow our checklist of duties down to "one thing" might prove to be challenging. Yet I'm convinced that if we don't do the "one thing," then we will never effectively accomplish the other things.

I suppose that we could argue over what should take precedence in our lives, but against the myriad of options that we could discuss, the Bible describes someone—two people

The One Thing

actually — who found the one thing. David made a request of the Lord — one thing that he asked, actually, of the Lord. His request was to dwell in the house of the Lord all the days of his life (Psalm 27:4).

The word "dwell" doesn't mean to make a casual visit with the Lord every now and then. It literally means to abide, remain, or to sit down with someone for a long, long time. Dwelling with the Lord describes a posture of intimacy. To know Him, to really know Him, we must cultivate a lifestyle that lives from His presence. God's acquaintance is rarely established through pop calls, but we must arrange our lives around His presence.

There were two things that David desired while seeking the presence of the Lord. First, he wanted to "behold" the beauty of the Lord. This word means more than merely looking at someone, it actually means to become "envisioned." David wanted to see with new eyes. He wanted His eyes opened. Let me say it this way: we can't see until we see! The moment that we look upon the Lord our eyes are truly opened. Our perspective changes when we look upon the Lord. Fear, anxiety, stress, and worry are not my focus. You will never have a proper perspective by watching CNN or Fox News. You'll never see clearly if you're watching your friends, the culture, or the latest media hype. Beholding the Lord is the only way to see everything else in its proper perspective.

Little wonder, then, that the writer of Hebrews said, "Fixing our eyes on Jesus, the author and perfecter of faith . . ." (Hebrews 12:2a). Faith will never be established by looking at anything else other than Jesus. Second, David desired to meditate in the Lord's presence. To "meditate" in this context means to inquire or investigate. He wanted direction for His life, and he realized that it would only come from the presence of the Lord.

Reflecting on the Lord's presence is the only way that we'll discover our next move. Direction comes from Him alone. His Spirit guides us into all truth (John 16:13). Outside of His presence we will be lost, confused, and disillusioned. Is your mind consumed with His presence these days?

In the New Testament Mary was at the feet of Jesus listening to every word He spoke (Luke 10:39). Martha, however, was not meditating on the Lord. We know that because she was worried and bothered about many things (Luke 10:41). Consequently, she became a source of distraction to Mary, who was doing the "one thing" that was necessary according to Jesus, and Martha wanted to uproot Mary's posture of intimacy.

Distracted people will distract people. Their distraction will always be used to influence people *from* the presence of the Lord. Someone like this on your ministry team, prayer team, or leadership team will cause everyone involved to drift from the presence of Christ. Because they haven't discovered the one thing in their lives, namely living in the presence of Jesus, they lead others away from the Word of the Lord. Martha essentially saw her activity of greater importance than listening to Jesus, so she requested that Jesus stop dispensing words of life so that Mary could help Martha with *her* ministry.

The One Thing

If you haven't found the one thing in your life, you will be distracted by the "many things," and most of them will lead you away from Jesus. No wonder there is so much burn-out and weariness in the church. We will never really know the Word outside of His presence. We won't see clearly, we won't have direction, and we'll find ourselves preoccupied with much worry and anxiety.

By calling us to the one thing, I'm not suggesting that we quit our jobs and shirk our daily responsibilities. People get the idea that dwelling in the presence of the Lord implies inactivity. I'm not taking away from those times in our lives when we retreat or spend a week in solitude with Jesus, but living in His presence is a posture of the heart. In the new covenant we become the sanctuary of the Holy Spirit (1 Corinthians 6:19), so it's possible to "sit at the feet" of Jesus while driving, cooking, or working in an assembly line.

His presence dwells within us so we're the walking house of the Lord that David requested to dwell in. We must learn to turn our affections toward Jesus every moment of each day. We must discover the joy and possibilities of living every moment out of intimacy with Christ. This is the one thing that will enable us to walk with purpose, power, and effectiveness. It's the one thing that will transform people around us with the fragrance of Christ. He's the one thing that will produce the many things, the essence of life that will generate abundant life.

PRAYER

There is only one thing that is necessary, Jesus, and I want to discover that in my life. Please remove all distractions from my life. I ask only that I may learn to dwell in your presence moment by moment, behold your beauty, and mediate on your Word, amen.

APPLICATION

1. Have you discovered that place of intimacy with Jesus?
2. What keeps you from a place of intimacy?
3. Can you describe what it means to live out of a place of intimacy?
4. What can you do to eliminate distraction in your life?

16

Borderless Faith (Part One)

Faith believes for things that are "out of bounds" and hopes for things that demand supernatural intervention.

I have come across people who believe God for things that seem "reasonable." Is that true faith? Faith by its very definition believes for things that are *not* just possible but for things that are impossible. If we only believe for things that are possible, then we're focused on the natural, and we're looking at what can be seen. The Bible tells us to look at what cannot be seen (2 Corinthians 4:18). Faith believes for things that are totally unreasonable in terms of natural explanations.

Faith believes for things that are "out of bounds" and hopes for things that demand supernatural intervention. As long as I can pull something off myself, there's no need for a divine touch. When I get to the place where I have no more options, then I'm stepping into the realm of faith. It's when I don't know what to do, where to turn, or how I'm going to make it that I rejoice the loudest because I've just entered the place where my faith is activated.

There's a story in the gospel of Mark that demonstrates the need for borderless faith. Jesus was approached by a man named Jairus who fell at Jesus' feet, which is the highest place to be, and said, "My little daughter is at the point of death; *please* come and lay Your hands on her, so that she will get well and live" (Mark 5:23b). Whether Jairus came on his own initiative or by the prodding of those in the synagogue that he represented, we don't know. But there was enough faith elicited in this desperate cry to have Jesus touch Jairus' sick daughter and bring total healing to her.

In the text there's a story within a story in verses 25 through 34 that personify faith. It's no accident that this story is wedged within the story of Jairus because Jesus' closing words in these verses were: "Daughter, your faith has made you well" (Mark 5:34b). One woman's faith exceeded the borders of everyone's faith in the crowd, and she was the only one, who we're aware of, who put a demand on the anointing that Jesus was hosting. Many people "touched" Jesus that day, but only one woman touched him with unlimited faith, and she was made whole. Twelve years of suffering came to an end because one woman refused to allow anything to stand in her way, and her tenacious faith pushed her beyond what was reasonable. She pressed beyond the ordinary, and, therefore, she experienced the extraordinary.

As Jesus was speaking to the woman who had been healed, some folks came from Jairus' house and said to him, "Your daughter has died; why trouble the Teacher anymore?"

(Mark 5:35b). Listen to the implication of that statement. If your daughter was merely sick, Jesus could heal her, but because she is dead, it's beyond His capacity to do anything. In other words, their faith had limits. They believed for what was reasonable in their minds. They believed for what was possible—namely, that sickness could be healed but nothing could be done about death. Raising the dead was beyond the borders of their faith, and, therefore, in their minds it was now pointless to involve Jesus.

Many people stop pressing into Jesus because they've agreed with their circumstances. Their reality is no greater than what they see with their natural eyes, so the idea of approaching Jesus with the impossible is outside the parameters of their limited faith. "And Jesus said to him, 'If You can?' All things are possible to him who believes" (Mark 9:23). I believe "all things" means all things, and nothing is impossible with God, so let's believe for things beyond the borders of our understanding.

I remember prophesying in the ear of a man who was brain dead because of an overdose of drugs. The functions of his body were being sustained by a machine, and everything in the natural realm screamed that this man was gone. Yet, God told me to prophesy life over this death-filled man. In twenty-four hours he came out of that traumatic situation, and I shared the good news of Jesus with him. I'm learning to live with borderless faith. I'm learning to trust God for what seems unreasonable because when the Son of Man comes, I want to be found with faith (Luke 18:8).

"But Jesus, overhearing what was being spoken said to the synagogue official [Jairus], 'Do not be afraid *any longer*, only believe'" (Mark 5:36). The word fear (*phobeo*) means to be in awe of something or to revere it. Fear can actually be a form of idolatry because we revere the circumstance more than we do Jesus. One expositor said this word *phobeo* means to flee or to be seized with fear to the point that we are scared away. In this case Jesus was telling Jairus, and those who came with the disparaging news, to not run or be scared away because of the situation. Jesus also said, "Only believe." The verb tense suggests that Jesus was telling them to "keep on believing." In other words, Jesus was stating the need to believe beyond borders. He wanted Jairus and his company to remain in faith no matter what the circumstances were, and Jesus desires the same for you and me.

What would you like Jesus to do: Redeem prodigals? Deliver someone from additions? Heal a terminal disease? Transform your city? Revive your church? Restore a broken marriage? Reach nations for Christ? I challenge you to ask God to take your faith beyond all borders and keep on believing no matter the circumstances.

Borderless Faith (Part One)

PRAYER

Jesus, I repent for agreeing with my circumstances. I repent for revering circumstances more than I do you. I align myself with your Word. Take my faith beyond the borders of the natural into the realm of the supernatural, amen.

APPLICATON

1. (Answer the questions from this lesson) What would you like Jesus to do in your life?
2. How would you define faith?
3. Is your faith being stretched beyond borders?
4. What kinds of things hinder you from believing the impossible?

17

Borderless Faith (Part Two)

When our faith is not borderless, we only believe for things that seem possible or reasonable.

In our last lesson, we discussed how Jesus was approached by a man named Jairus who wanted Jesus to come lay His hands on his daughter to heal her. She was at the point of death, so Jairus elicited the help of Jesus. Jesus left at once to heal her; however, He was delayed in the process by a desperate, faith-filled woman. While many people were pressing in on Jesus, there was no indication that they were being significantly changed. This woman's faith, however, led her to believe: "For she thought, 'If I just touch His garments, I will get well'" (Mark 5:28).

Perhaps she had heard about the people being healed and pressing against Jesus on other occasions (Mark 3:10). Maybe she believed the prophecy that says, "But for you who fear My name, the sun of righteousness will arise with

Borderless Faith (Part Two)

healing in its wings; . . ." (Malachi 4:2a). The Hebrew word for wings (*kanaph*) refers to the corner of a garment or the border of a cloth. Another version of this same story states that she touched the "fringe of His cloak" (Luke 8:44). It doesn't matter what prompted her, the point is that she possessed no limits to her faith. It was a divine interruption demonstrating to Jairus that we should never stop believing.

As Jesus commended this woman for her faith, some people approached Jairus with dreaded news. "But Jesus, overhearing what was being spoken, said to the synagogue official [Jairus], 'Do not be afraid *any longer*, only believe'" (Mark 5:36). In other words, Jesus was exhorting him to not revere, to be in awe of, or to run away (the meaning of being afraid) because of the news that was just delivered to him. Jesus challenged him to keep on believing no matter what the circumstances were. To Jesus, raising the dead is no more difficult than healing a sick body. It's only more difficult in our minds.

When our faith is not borderless, we only believe for things that seem possible or reasonable. The people who reported to Jairus didn't want to involve Jesus anymore because Jairus' daughter had died. In their minds Jesus was only needed when sickness was the issue but not death. Their faith had limits.

I'm challenged by the fact that Jesus only allowed Peter, James, and John to accompany Him to Jairus' house. Perhaps the other disciples possessed limited faith. I wonder if I would have been invited to accompany Jesus had I been there. Wouldn't it be sobering if Jesus requested that we not go with Him because our limited faith would become a hindrance?

When Jesus reached the house the Bible says, "He saw a commotion, and *people* loudly weeping and wailing" (Mark 5:38b). The word commotion (*thorubos*) means noisy confusion, an uproar, and agitation due to troubled minds. A common practice in this culture was to hire mourners, but the commotion was aroused because of faithlessness. Note what Jesus said: "Why make a commotion and weep?" (Mark 5:39a). In other words, what happened to your faith? Believers and churches who lack faith will always be thrown into agitation and confusion during a crisis.

Jesus continued, "The child has not died, but is asleep" (Mark 5:39b). Think about that statement for a moment. Paul wrote, "But having the same spirit of faith, according to what is written, 'I believed, therefore I spoke,' we also believe, therefore we also speak" (2 Corinthians 4:13). Paul was quoting the Psalmist who possessed faith in the midst of great challenges.

Faith is the capacity to see beyond the immediate to the ultimate, to see beyond the natural into the supernatural; therefore, we don't react to *what is*, but we declare *what will be*. If we speak from a posture of faith, we are speaking from the realm we're focused on—the spiritual realm, and that realm is filled with unlimited blessings (Ephesians 1:3).

Jesus looked beyond the natural circumstances, that Jairus' daughter was dead, and He saw this girl through the perspective of faith. He saw a resurrection. He didn't see death. He believed; therefore, He spoke. When the faithless crowd heard His statement, they began to laugh and deride Him. Don't be surprised when those around you criticize and scoff your unlimited faith. If you're surrounded by people who are consumed by this world's cares, problems, and realities, they will laugh at your faith-filled declarations.

Having put them out of the house, Jesus took the child by the hand and said, ". . . Get up" (Mark 5:41b). She immediately got up and walked around, and those who witnessed that miracle were "completely astounded" (Mark 5:42b). Some scholars define "completely astounded" as standing outside of your mind or going beyond the imagination. That definition sounds like borderless faith, doesn't it?

A renewed mind, one that thinks beyond the possible toward the impossible, is one that is set "on things above, not on things that are on earth" (Colossians 3:2). We have a God that goes beyond what we ask *or imagine* (Ephesians 3:20).

What would your life look like if you possessed borderless faith? My challenge to you, and to me, is to keep on believing no matter what the circumstances are. And if and when we walk through adversity, let's look beyond what is and see what will be. Let's learn to see from a heavenly perspective. I want to please my Father with that kind of faith (Hebrews 11:6). Will you ask for a renewed mind? Will you ask that Jesus increases your faith beyond all borders?

PRAYER

Jesus, take our minds beyond the immediate into the ultimate. Increase our faith beyond all borders so that we'll always believe, regardless of the circumstances. Enable us to believe even when we're being laughed at. We choose to set our minds on things above, amen.

APPLICATION

1. Are you willing to doing whatever it takes to press into the hem of the garment of Jesus?
2. In what ways do you see your faith building as you ask God for an increase of faith?
3. What boundaries do you typically put on yourself that is not the representation of faith?

18

Believe, Then Speak

Faith is not merely the assurance of what's hoped for, but it is the conviction or proof of what's not yet been seen.

How different would your life be if you only spoke from a posture of faith?

In the last two lessons, I've written about borderless faith, probably because God is trying to teach me something very essential. I want to remain in the same vein of thinking with this lesson. The Bible says, "But having the same spirit of faith, according to what is written, 'I believed, therefore I spoke,' we also believe, therefore we also speak" (2 Corinthians 4:13). Paul indicated that we're to speak from a posture of faith. We believe; therefore, we speak. Statements that we make should be declarations of what we believe, not laments of what has failed to happen. Our language should reflect our faith.

Too often we become overwhelmed by surrounding circumstances: the economy, sickness, crime, failures, sin, or disease, and if we're not careful, these issues begin to become the center of our conversations. In other words, the nature of our language starts to reflect the content of this world: it revolves around earthly issues. This shift gives way to grumbling and complaining—something that we're commanded *not* to do (Philippians 2:14), not to mention that it increases false beliefs.

While I'm not suggesting that we ignore people or avoid conversations, I *am* suggesting that we heed the exhortation that says, "Let no unwholesome word proceed from your mouth, but only such *a word* as is good for edification according to the *need of the moment*, so that it will give grace to those who hear" (Ephesians 4:29).

An impartation of grace usually doesn't occur when we ruminate on the brokenness of our world. We impart grace when we see our world—our city—through the lens of faith. What would our cities look like if a sweeping revival ignited them? What would it look like if a massive outpouring of the Holy Spirit fell on our communities? To merely define the sin of your city is to fall short of becoming an ambassador for Christ (2 Corinthians 5:20). Looking at your city from the perspective of faith will lead you to pray for it with passion and fervor, and additionally it will place you in a position to minister to those you are praying for.

My wife and I have been praying for our neighbors, and we've been following the Holy Spirit in ways to minister to them. However, they are far from God, and their lifestyles reflect that fact. Cindy and I look beyond what we see to what they can be through the redemptive grace of

Jesus Christ. Our conversations are not laments of their condition, but rather we are speaking about them from the perspective of faith. We believe; therefore, we speak. We have faith that they'll be redeemed, set free, and become leaders in our church, so our language about them reflects the focus of our hearts.

The infamous "faith chapter" in the Bible begins with this: "Now faith is the assurance of *things* hoped for, the conviction of things not seen" (Hebrews 11:1). Assurance can be defined as a foundation or something that has substance. Faith has substance to it. We actually "stand on" what we hope for because it's that real to us. In this same chapter, we read about Moses: "By faith, he left Egypt, not fearing the wrath of the king; for he endured, as seeing Him who is unseen" (Hebrews 11:27).

How was Moses able to endure? He saw something that very few others around him saw. His faith gave him a foundation to stand upon, and he wasn't going to be moved by anything. Faith is not merely the assurance of what's hoped for, but it is the conviction or proof of what's not yet been seen. The BBE translation reads: "The sign that the things not seen are true." Faith proves itself. When you read chapter eleven of Hebrews in its entirety, you discover many men and woman who proved the reality of their faith. Every person stood on what they hoped for.

If we live by faith, we will see things long before they are a reality. We will see families reunited, marriages restored, prodigals saved, believers sanctified, bodies healed, churches revived, and cities transformed. What we see will determine what we speak. Jesus, from the perspective of the kingdom of God, decreed over a sinful city: "Behold, I say to you, lift up your eyes and look on the fields, that they are white for harvest" (John 4:35).

He looked at a mountain in Caesarea Philippi, the very place where pagan worship occurred hundreds of years before that moment, and He said, "I also say to you that you are Peter, and upon this rock I will build my church; and the gates of Hades will not overpower it" (Matthew 16:18). Jesus saw with a kingdom viewpoint; therefore, He spoke. What do you see? How do you view your neighborhood, church, or city? Maybe the question should be: What kinds of things come out of your mouth? What you say might be an indicator of what you see.

Faith comes from hearing the Word of Christ (Romans 10:17). Let's remain close to Him. Let's stay at Jesus' feet like Mary and listen to His Word (Luke 10:39). No matter what we might walk through, my prayer is that when we come to the end of our earthly journey, we will say, as Paul said, "I have fought the good fight, I have finished the course, I have kept our faith" (2 Timothy 4:7). But until then, let's learn to see with eyes of faith and speak with mouths filled with kingdom declarations.

PRAYER

God, I repent for gripes, complaints, and negativity. Increase my faith and help me to see my world from the perspective of faith. Let my mouth become an instrument of praise and a voice of hope. Let my words impart grace to all I speak to, in Jesus' name, amen.

APPLICATION

1. Read through Hebrews 11 a couple times per day.
2. How will your perspective for a situation change when you look at it through faith eyes?
3. What do you believe for with kingdom-minded faith? (Salvation of family members, city-wide transformation, healing, etc.)
4. Do you have greater faith for others than yourself? Why or why not?
5. In what ways can you give more time to staying in the Word for faith-filled answers instead of depending on your mind to solve the problem?

19
No Shrinking Back

Faith gives you the understanding that everything you see with your natural eyes is inferior to the kingdom realm.

Do you know what is opposite to faith?

I'll answer that question in a moment. Paul wrote, "Therefore we do not lose heart, but though our outer man is decaying, yet our inner man is being renewed day by day. For our momentary, light affliction is producing for us an eternal weight of glory far beyond all comparison" (2 Corinthians 4:16–17).

Our momentary, light affliction? This is coming from a guy who was beaten with rods, stoned, shipwrecked, sleep deprived, hungered and thirsted, and exposed to the cold and who spent his life in danger of thieves, gentiles, and false brethren (2 Corinthians 11:23–28). He called those experiences "momentary, light afflictions."

I often picture myself sitting around a campfire in heaven one day, listening to various martyrs share their stories. John the Baptist would talk of his beheading, Peter would talk of his upside-down crucifixion, the faithful saints of Hebrews chapter eleven would share their stories, and the apostle Paul would finish with his sundry of persecutions. Then I picture one of them asking me, "Hey Rob, what were some things you endured?" That would be a moment of embarrassment for me at this point in my life because I have found myself complaining about superfluous things.

Afflictions for some of us are traffic jams, lukewarm coffee, and long lines at a checkout. I want to mature in my walk with Jesus to the point that nothing upsets me, and it doesn't matter who likes me or dislikes me, what I have or what I've lost, or what level of insults, adversity, or persecution that I may experience. I want to get to the place to where I'm able to call the tribulations of my life momentary, light afflictions.

I believe the secret to living with such extraordinary peace like Paul did is found in his next statement. He wrote, "While we look not at the things which are seen, but at the things which are not seen; for the things which are seen are temporal, but the things which are not seen are eternal" (2 Corinthians 4:18). Paul was describing the essence of faith. "Now faith is the assurance of *things* hoped for, the conviction of things not seen" (Hebrews 11:1).

Faith is the capacity to see what you can't see because it gives you an eternal perspective. Faith gives you the understanding that everything you see with your natural eyes is inferior to the kingdom realm. When you live by faith, nothing in the earthly realm overwhelms you because your trust abides in the heavenly realm. This is how Moses endured. He was able to *see* into the realm of the kingdom, and he saw Him who was unseen (Hebrews 11:27).

What, then, is opposite to faith? The answer is "sight." The moment that our natural eyes take notice of what happens in the earthly realm, we will, as Paul declared, "lose heart." I'm not suggesting that we walk around with our eyes closed, and neither was Paul. The point is to open our spiritual eyes. We are to look at what is unseen. Our eyes are to remain fixed in the heavenly realm. We are to look only unto Jesus (Hebrews 12:2). When we merely live by our natural sight, we will lose heart (*enkakeo*). This compound word means to become discouraged, disheartened, and overwhelmed by fear. Does that describe your life?

According to the Bible, a righteous person will live by faith (Hebrews 10:38). That means that we don't live by feelings, emotions, reactions, people, circumstances, fear, or adversities. Everything that we experience on this side of eternity is for a purpose. "For momentary, light affliction is producing for us an eternal weight of glory far beyond all comparison" (2 Corinthians 4:17). Expositors liken this verse to an eternal bank account that builds interest over the years, and one day the full weight of God's glory will rest upon us. To experience the full measure of the glory of God is truly beyond all comparison.

Living by faith and not by sight is the eternal perspective that views all of life as but an inch on an endless rope. The remaining length of rope represents eternity. Therefore, anything that we might endure is light and momentary. In the grand scheme of things, what happens *to* us is not as important as what happens *in* us. When our sight is set on eternal matters, we are going to be renewed day by day. We grow with courage, perseverance, endurance, and spiritual passion.

When we live by faith, we will not shrink back (Hebrews 10:38). We will not cower, withdraw, or quit. To shrink back actually means "to cease from declaring." In other words, to shrink back means that we no longer speak with hope. Our conversations, then, become fear driven and filled with complaints, negativity, and gripes. Language such as that indicates that we are living by sight and not by faith. Isn't it time to set your eyes on things above and not on the things of this earth? Decide today that you will never shrink back because you've opened your *real* eyes to what really matters.

PRAYER

God, I pray that you would open my eyes. Give me a spirit of wisdom and revelation. Remove the veil from my eyes so that I can begin to see what matters most. Enable me, by faith, to never shrink back. I pray in Jesus' name, amen.

APPLICATION

1. What are some areas that you need the Holy Spirit to help you overcome?
2. Think about how you see things. Do you see them through an earthly lens or a heavenly perspective?
3. Are you influenced by situations or circumstances around you? Do you stand strong in who you are, or do you shrink back to fit in with those around you?
4. Condition yourself to set your mind on things above throughout this day, and train yourself to look with faith at whatever comes against you.

20

Word Versus Circumstances

Obedience to the Word is our only option in a love relationship with Jesus.

The Word of God is powerful when we trust and obey it. Jesus was teaching the multitudes from a boat. "When He had finished speaking, He said to Simon, 'Put out into the deep water and let down your nets for a catch'" (Luke 5:4). It's interesting to note that the word deep (*bathos*) describes something more than depth of water. One expositor says that this word indicates a profound depth in the mind of God.

In other words, Jesus was inviting Simon into deeper things spiritually. He wanted Simon to experience a depth of God that he wasn't aware of at the moment. Let me suggest that obedience to the Word always brings us into deeper experiences with God. Of course, in the context of the story, obeying Jesus' Word meant moving from where they were to deeper waters and letting down every net available.

The beginning of verse 5 is humorous to me: "Simon answered . . ." Jesus wasn't asking a question! He made a statement and expected instant obedience. I'm amazed at how often we turn Jesus' statements into questions, and then we try to reason with Him. Obedience to the Word is our only option in a love relationship with Jesus.

Simon went on to explain to Jesus that they had been toiling all night and caught nothing. In other words, Simon was responding from his unhappy experience from fishing. He wanted Jesus to realize that from *his* perspective, launching out into the deep to catch fish would be of no benefit. Allow me to insert the following: I've prayed about that before; I've put my faith in that and it didn't work; I've sought God about that situation and got no response; or I've asked for healing and it didn't happen. Each of these statements reflects our tendency to place trust in our experience over and above what Christ might be asking us to do. In reality, we're manifesting our unbelief in His Word by putting confidence in our failed circumstances.

I have had people explain to me that they've gone to the altar during an invitation, seeking to be healed, and nothing happened to them. So, they reduced God's Word on the subject of healing and redefined it to match their limited situation. Bob Sorge said, "Belief in God's Word to heal gives him the incentive and momentum to continue pursuing God." Sorge has been waiting and trusting God for his own healing but refuses to quit pursuing God on the matter because of what the Bible says.

Word Versus Circumstances

My friend Craig Rench told me about a woman who went forward to be healed fifty times when nothing happened to her, but on the fifty-first time she was instantly healed. What would have happened if she placed greater faith in her circumstances than in the Word of God? My guess is that she would have quit pressing into God after about three or four times, and she probably wouldn't have been healed. We must always trust God's Word over our circumstances no matter how long we have labored.

Simon Peter conceded in tossing the net overboard, and it was filled with more fish than it could hold. Simon fell at Jesus' feet in repentance, realizing that he could have missed the blessing if he had failed to obey Jesus.

There is an interesting bit of insight to this story that some scholars underscore. Some translations state that Jesus told Simon Peter to let down the "nets" (*diktua*) which is a plural, yet Simon only cast out one "net" (*diktoun*), a singular noun. It appears that Simon, in his reluctance to trust Jesus' Word, only partially obeyed Jesus, and he adjusted Jesus' words to fit his lack of faith. In that case, Simon *really* missed a blessing.

We can only imagine the amount of fish Peter would have caught had there been three or four nets in the water. If we allow our experiences to define what is possible, then we'll miss what God might want to do in and through our lives. We must not reduce the Word or redefine it to fit our context. The Word of God will always trump our experiences if we trust Him.

The context of this story, however, is about reaching people. Jesus was commissioning Simon to catch people instead of fish. How will we ever reach people for God if we can't place total faith in what He says? I was prompted by the Holy Spirit one time while at a restaurant to speak to someone about the Lord. That initial prompting was met with a bit of questioning and resistance because of a failed attempt a time before when I was shut down and told that they were not interested in what I was "peddling." That has rarely happened to me, but the memory was still fresh in my mind when I sensed the leading of the Lord.

Yet, not only does the Bible tell us to announce the good news to the world (Mark 16:15), but I was hearing the *living* Word commissioning me. Following the voice, I threw the net out, and this person made a profession of faith right in the middle of a busy restaurant. I'm not advocating that we're to be obnoxious, pushy, and insensitive. Quite the contrary, I'm advocating that we *always* listen to the written and living Word of God.

I believe that there are people to be caught for the Lord, but it will only happen if we venture into deeper waters with Jesus and throw every net into the world. Don't let circumstances dictate your lifestyle or failed attempts at serving God hinder your obedience. Trust the Word at all times. "And Jesus said to Simon, 'Do not fear, from now on you will be catching men'" (Luke 5:10).

PRAYER

Lord, help me to listen and obey the Word moment by moment by moment, amen.

APPLICATION

1. How quickly are you influenced by the circumstances that rise up around you? Do they typically hinder or strengthen your faith?
2. Does your lifestyle consistently trust in God's Word? Do you obey His leadership instantly?
3. Can you devote more time to reading and studying the Word? What are some things that you might be able to give up in order to spend more time in the Word of God?

21
Living with a Kingdom Mindset

Setting our mind on things above doesn't guarantee that we won't experience adversity; rather, it means that we're able to see over it.

Several years ago, I was driving to the airport through pelting rain and sleet to depart for a ministry trip. As the airplane took off through the gray overcast skies, it wasn't long before we broke through the cloud layers. We emerged into what looked to be a totally different day, and I was taken back by the beauty of the bright sunshine. That same day seemed to possess two different realities.

What reality do you usually live in? Listen to these words from the apostle Paul: "Therefore if you have been raised up with Christ, keep seeking the things above, where Christ is, seated at the right hand of God. Set your mind on the things above, not on the things that are on earth" (Colossians. 3:1–2).

We are to "keep seeking" (*zeteo*). This present tense verb means to keep inquiring, investigating, looking, considering, and examining. If you have been raised to life by the power of Christ, then you are to live by constantly looking above. You should never take your eyes off Jesus, which means that you should consistently view life from heaven's perspective. Your line of sight should always contain the kingdom of God.

Paul continued by saying, "Set your mind" (*phroneo*). This is also a present tense verb that means to constantly direct one's attention and affections toward something. According to this verse we are to constantly direct our attention toward Jesus. Truly, whatever has your attention governs your actions.

What does it mean to live each day directing our attention to things above and not to the things of earth? How do we maintain a job, raise children, pay bills, resolve conflicts, and manage life while looking into heaven? My first response is short and simple: one cannot do anything well on earth if they aren't focused on heaven. This means that every thought must be taken captive and viewed from heaven's perspective (2 Corinthians 10:5).

Don't dwell on things that aren't pleasing to Jesus. Otherwise, our minds will be held hostage by what's happening around us, and eventually we will be filled with fear, frustration, anxiety, and every poisonous thing we've opened our mind to that's contrary to Christ. Setting our mind on things above doesn't guarantee that we won't experience adversity, but it means that we're able to see over it. It means that we're living above the circumstances and not under them.

A kingdom mindset is focused on Christ more than anything or anyone else. Every thought is shaped with His presence in mind. Getting even more practical, it means considering what Jesus thinks about things more than how *we* think. We do that by simply asking Him: Jesus, what do you think about my children's behavior? Jesus, how would you handle this problem? Jesus, what should I do about that troublesome person? Jesus, what should I say to my boss?

My friend Hal Perkins calls this kind of lifestyle being discipled by Jesus. We are integrating Him into every activity, conversation, and decision that we make. We are doing life with Jesus every moment of every day. That is how we become "one flesh" with Christ just as He prayed (John 17:21).

Think about Paul's words in Colossians 3:3, "For you have died and your life is hidden with Christ in God." If we have died, then life isn't about us. It doesn't matter what *we* think, what *we* say, what *our* opinion is, or what *our* response should be. We are supposed to be dead! We are to be concealed in Christ. That means He's to be seen and heard through us.

The truth is that none of us have been built to handle life on our own. We were created to function in union with Jesus Christ, and, therefore, we should view all of life from His perspective, not ours. Apart from Him we can't do anything (John 15:5). Paul wrote these sobering words: "For many walk, of whom I often told you, and now tell you even weeping, *that they are* enemies of the cross of Christ, *whose* end is their destruction, whose god is *their* appetite, and *whose* glory is in their shame, who set their minds on earthly things" (Philippians 3:18-19).

Note what Paul wrote, "Who set their minds on earthly things." This is why I believe that he wept. He saw people consumed more by the earthly realm—which is but a blip on the radar—than the eternal realm. In actuality, if we are shaped more by this realm than the kingdom of heaven, then we become enemies of the cross.

We are to live as ambassadors of Christ here on earth (2 Corinthians 5:20). That means we belong to another country. We represent heaven while living and working here on earth for a period of time because our true citizenship belongs in another realm (Philippians 3:20).

Therefore, our thinking is to be fashioned by heaven's values and not things here on earth. It's really the only way to bring heaven to earth as Jesus prayed (Luke 11:2). When our minds are fixed on Christ and molded around heaven's values, we're able to release His presence to those around us. Living with our minds on Christ keeps us in a posture to minister effectively no matter where we are.

Sometimes people push back by responding, "You don't understand what I have to deal with. My life is too complicated to always remain focused on Jesus." The reality is, however, that Jesus desires to be in the midst of everything we do. A kingdom mindset doesn't avoid life nor does it neglect responsibilities; rather, it involves Christ into all of our daily affairs. A kingdom mindset takes Jesus into the mess and complications of our lives, and it integrates Him into everything that we do by seeking His direction, guidance, and wisdom.

Set your mind on things above. Seek Him and His kingdom first and foremost (Matthew 6:33). Let Jesus saturate your thinking. Continue living with a kingdom mindset rather than an earthly mindset. If you do, you'll probably see the sun more than the rain.

PRAYER

Lord, I desire to live from a kingdom mindset. Help me to take every thought captive and cast away the thoughts that are not of you — only filling my mind with your thoughts.

APPLICATION

1. What things distract you from living with a kingdom mindset?
2. How much of your day is viewing things from an earthly perspective instead of from a kingdom mindset?
3. Is Jesus at the center of all you do? All your decisions, thoughts, and choices?

22
The Power of Hearing

As believers we aren't to be an echo of our culture but a voice from the kingdom.

Most of you have read the passage where a woman interrupted Jesus as he taught. She "raised her voice and said to Him, 'Blessed is the womb that bore You and the breasts at which You nursed'" (Luke 11:27b).

I've had many interruptions during my messages, but nothing like what this woman did. From what I can observe in the text, Jesus responded rather quickly. "But He said, 'On the contrary, blessed are those who hear the word of God and observe it'" (Luke 11:28). To be "blessed" literally means to be in the right position or alignment with God to receive His favor. Blessing and favor comes to those, Jesus said, when they "hear the word."

Think about this for a moment, what would be the opposite of that statement? If blessing comes by hearing, obviously

The Power of Hearing

there are some serious consequences for *not* hearing. I can't begin to describe the mess that I've caused when I acted on good assumptions rather than waiting to hear His Word on the matter.

Blessings come when we hear the Word and, then, when we "observe" it, Jesus said. To observe means to keep, defend, or even to produce what we hear. So, we're not merely hearers of the Word, but we are doers, too (James 1:22). But I want to underscore hearing in this lesson because I believe what we do or say should be contingent upon what we hear. Who or what are you listening to these days?

One of the most essential things that we are to do as Spirit-filled people is to listen. Jesus was asked what commandment was foremost of all. His answer may surprise you because most of us respond with loving Him with all of our heart, soul, mind, and strength. And that's true, we should love Him with all of our being and even neighbors as we love ourselves. But Jesus' answer to the question actually began with something else.

"Jesus answered, 'The foremost commandment is, "Hear, O Israel! . . ."'" (Mark 12:29). I have skipped over that for years—maybe because I wasn't listening. But if you think about it, the ability to love God and people is generated in our willingness to listen to God. How we listen to Him is reflected in how we listen to and treat people. Usually we reflect the characteristics of the one we give most of our attention to. I want to be an imitator of God (Ephesians 5:1). That means I must give my attention to Him so that I can replicate His character.

James wrote, "In the exercise of His will He brought us forth by the word of truth, so that we would be a kind of first fruits among His creatures" (James 1:18). The phrase "brought forth" means to give birth to something. So, every person was birthed into being because the Word of God was declared. In fact, all of creation was brought forth because God spoke! There is extraordinary power in the declaration of the Word. We carry life and death in the words that we speak (Proverbs 18:21).

What you say can raise people up, or it can destroy them. What are you listening to because that's probably what you're repeating? If you stuff your ears with the wrong content, you may be declaring deadly words over those that you speak to. Give your ears to the Lord. Listen to Him more than you listen to anyone else. So, when James continued with, "Everyone must be quick to hear," he was referring to our readiness to hear the Word of God.

Paul encouraged us all to desire the manifestation of prophecy (1 Corinthians 14:1). The simplest definition of prophecy is to speak what we hear the Lord saying to us. In other words, He speaks, we hear, and then we release what He has spoken. Truly, every believer can prophesy because every believer can hear the Lord speak (John 10:27).

What if, however, we are *not* hearing the Lord's words, but we are hearing everyone else's words? When you fill your head with CNN or the latest string of gossip, you might be repeating those same words when you speak. In a sense, you *are* prophesying, but it's negative, harmful, and lacks redemptive grace (Colossians 4:6).

The Power of Hearing

Perhaps a doctor just gave you a report from your latest exam. Before you "give ear" to those words, get alone with Jesus and listen to His words on the matter. Otherwise, you may be speaking things over your life that people say and not what God says. As believers we aren't to be an echo of our culture but a voice from the kingdom. The flesh profits nothing, Jesus said. We are to speak as He did with words filled with spirit and life (John 6:63).

Hearing and listening are so essential in our relationship with Christ. Jesus *only* spoke what He heard His Father say (John 12:50). Perhaps that is the reason His words caused blind eyes to open, deaf ears to unstop, mute tongues to talk, crippled limbs to straighten, and dead bodies to raise to life. Jesus was an anointed leader because He was a dedicated listener. He heard what the Father wanted, and He did and said accordingly. Our spiritual lives should be molded in our willingness to hear.

Practice listening to His voice throughout the day and speak, and do, only as He prompts. If you're a pastor or leader of a church, take time in your services to really hear Him. Perhaps He wants to move in a way that was unplanned. Surrender your service plan to His voice and watch what God can do.

The writer of Hebrews said, "Today if you hear His voice, Do not harden your hearts" (Hebrews 4:7b). The operative word in that statement is "if" you hear His voice. I don't think it's a matter of Him speaking to us. I believe that it's a matter of us actually taking the initiative to hear Him.

Listen to His voice today. What's He saying?

PRAYER

God, train me to listen more to your voice. Let the still quiet things permeate loudly in the heavenlies. Teach me how to be tuned to your voice in order to quickly obey what you are speaking. I want to hear everything that you have to speak, amen.

APPLICATION

1. What voice are you listening to as you walk through your day?
2. What kinds of things hinder you from hearing the voice of the Holy Spirit?
3. What kinds of things enhance your ability to hear the Lord?
4. Take time this week to be still and listen intently for the voice of the Lord. If you can, journal what you believe the Lord is saying to you.

23

Dull of Hearing

Too many congregations rely solely on the pastor to teach when truly all believers, if they are pressing into the Word, can instruct each other.

After explaining that we were brought forth by the Word, James continued by stating that everyone must be quick to hear (James 1:19). The context of this verse implies that we are to be quick to hear the Word. According to Jesus, we are blessed when we hear the Word (Luke 11:28). Can we become even *more* sensitive to the Word? I believe that we can, but I also believe that we can become dull of hearing.

This problem was evident for the believers in the epistle of Hebrews. After explaining that Christ had become the source of eternal salvation in the order of Melchizedek, the writer paused in his message and stated, "Concerning him we have much to say, and *it is* hard to explain, since you have become dull of hearing" (Hebrews 5:11).

Imagine if a pastor stood and said, "I'm having a problem teaching this message today, but the problem is not in my ability to explain it. The problem is with your ability to hear it because you've become insensitive." The original readers of this epistle were not in a position to grasp what was being said because their minds had become sluggish. The word dull (*nothros*) carries the idea of being lazy, slothful, or hard of hearing. So, at one time they were eager and hungry to hear, but over time they became dull of hearing and could no longer grasp deep truths.

Hebrews 5:12–14 highlights four characteristics of dullness of hearing. First, we fail to reach our spiritual potential. The writer said, "For though by this time you ought to be teachers, . . ." (Hebrews 5:12). This meant that they should have grown in the Word to the point that they could instruct others. Too many congregations rely solely on the pastor to teach when truly all believers, if they are pressing into the Word, can instruct each other.

Paul said, "When you assemble, each one has a psalm, has a teaching, has a revelation, has a tongue, has an interpretation. Let all things be done for edification" (1 Corinthians 14:26b). If believers are maturing in the Word and filled with the Spirit, then all can and should minister to each other.

Truly, all can edify each other and impart instruction if we're growing up in the Word. This does not override the responsibility of spiritual leaders but underscores the necessity to grow up in the Word so that all of us can spiritually edify and influence others. The audience in the book of

Hebrews had become dull of hearing and so failed to reach their potential to be a spiritual influence.

Second, we are unable to digest deep spiritual truths. "For though by this time you ought to be teachers, you have need again for someone to teach you the elementary principles of the oracles of God, you have come to need milk and not solid food" (Hebrews 5:12b). If we don't grow up in the Word, then we'll have to dumb-down our messages so that they're understood.

I'm astonished by the inability of many congregations to grasp messages about the Holy Spirit, kingdom principles, and the conduct of holiness. I've encountered the blank stares too many times when I've taught about laying on of hands, the resurrection of the dead, and aspects of eternal judgement—and those things are actually considered elementary doctrines (Hebrews 6:1-2).

Paul wrote that the Holy Spirit revealed the deep things of God, but if we're not pursuing an intimate relationship with the Spirit and consuming His Word, then we're going to have to settle for a child's portion of spiritual food.

Third, we live as spiritual infants. If we can only stomach spiritual milk instead of the word of righteousness, then we'll remain immature infants (Hebrews 5:13-14). The word infant (*nepios*) refers to a childish person. Nothing is worse than a church filled with immature, childish believers.

The church in Corinth was filled with jealousy, strife, and fleshly manifestations because the believers failed to grow up (1 Corinthians 3:1-3). Show me a church filled with immature Christians who should know better, and I'll show you a church filled with people who can't forgive, are easily offended, and will create divisions within the body of Christ. Their words, posts, and actions are toxic and nonredemptive. It's time for believers to leave the elementary teaching about Christ and press on toward maturity (Hebrews 6:1).

Fourth, we are unable to discern accurately between good and evil. Immature, dull believers are gullible and "... tossed here and there by waves and carried about by every wind of doctrine, ..." (Ephesians 4:14a). There's a vast difference between "good" and God, but if we're dull of hearing concerning the Word, then we'll become insensitive to the subtleties of evil that are so pervasive in our culture.

I'm heartbroken by the stories I hear of pastors, leaders, and Christians falling prey to the sundry of evil enticements. Only those who remain sensitive to the voice of the Holy Spirit and invest themselves in the Word of God will be able to examine all things and discern good from evil (1 Thessalonians 5:21).

My challenge in this lesson is for us to incline our ears to the Lord. Let's press into Him and listen to what He says so that we can live (Isaiah 55:3). Let's intentionally position ourselves at the feet of Jesus like Mary and listen to every word that proceeds from His mouth (Luke 10:39).

Keep turning unto the Lord so that He can remove the veil from our spiritual eyes and give us a spirit of wisdom and revelation (2 Corinthians 3:16; Ephesians 1:17). Then, with an unveiled face, we can all be transformed from glory to glory (2 Corinthians 3:18).

PRAYER

Jesus, I press into your heart to listen to your Word. Save me from becoming dull of hearing, in your name, amen.

APPLICATION

1. Are the words that you are speaking what you are hearing form a position of intimacy with the Father? Are they encouraging and life giving to those around you?
2. What are some of the outside influences that can dull the voice of God in your life? Do you need to change or adapt these in your life?
3. What is your current position in listening to Jesus? At His feet? In the room? Left Him at church on Sunday?

24

Holiness

Holiness becomes a lifestyle of seeking direction from the heavenly realm and not from earthly sources.

I believe it's not only possible to walk in holiness, but it's imperative. Recently, I had the privilege to teach a college-level course Doctrine of Holiness in Texas. I'm challenged by the Scriptures that paint a picture of what it looks like to walk in holiness. There are many Scriptures to choose from, but let's examine a passage from Colossians.

Paul wrote, "Therefore if you have been raised up with Christ, keep seeking the things above, where Christ is, seated at the right hand of God. Set your mind on the things above, not on the things that are on earth. For you have died and your life is hidden with Christ in God" (Colossians 3:1-3). These verses describe a holiness lifestyle in several ways.

First, we all need to be raised up because we were dead in our sins and transgressions (Ephesians 2:1-6). At one time, prior to Christ's intervention, we walked according to the course of this world. Our natures were corrupt, and we indulged the desires of the flesh. But even while we were in that condition, Christ Jesus made us alive, raised us up, and seated us in the heavenly realms in Him.

Holiness, then, becomes a position of intimacy seated in Christ Jesus "far above all rule and authority and power and dominion, . . ." (Ephesians 1:21). It's a lifestyle of prevailing over sin, Satan, and the works of darkness.

Secondly, because we're seated in Christ, we are to constantly seek things above. We're able to fulfill Jesus' directive: "But seek first His kingdom and His righteousness, and all these things will be added to you" (Matthew 6:33). This means that we are able to live without fear, worry, and anxiety because everything we need is supplied in Christ—the One whom our eyes are fixed on (Hebrews 12:2). Holiness becomes a lifestyle of seeking direction from the heavenly realm and not from earthly sources.

Third, our mind is set on things above and not on the things of this earth. We have a renewed mind that doesn't get consumed and overwhelmed by the things around us. We don't become distracted by the immediate because our minds are set on the ultimate. We are able to live in "perfect peace" because we have minds that are stayed on the Lord (Isaiah 26:3). We don't allow anything to rule our minds other than the peace of Christ (Colossians 3:15). Holiness becomes a lifestyle of rest and peace because we don't live in reaction to earthly circumstances.

Fourth, Paul indicated that we have died, and our life is now hidden with Christ. The only way that we will ever walk in holiness is by dying to our sinfulness and selfishness. We have to die to ourselves. Christianity is not about us, but it's about Christ. We die and get out of the picture so that He lives through us and can be seen. Paul stated, "I have been crucified with Christ; and it is no longer I who live, but Christ lives in me . . ." (Galatians 2:20a). Holiness is dying to your life and letting Christ become your life.

Because we've died in Christ, we also die to immorality, impurity, passion, evil desires, and greed (Colossians 3:5). We put aside things like anger, wrath, malice, slander, and abusive speech from our mouth (Colossians 3:8). This means that the only things coming out of our mouth are helpful, beneficial, and edifying toward others (Ephesians 4:29). We would never gossip or malign others in what we write or say because our speech is always filled with grace (Colossians 4:6). We're hidden in Christ so people don't hear us but Jesus through us when we talk, and, like Jesus, our words are filled with life (John 6:63).

When we die to ourselves and become hidden with Christ, new characteristics start to manifest in our lives, such as compassion, kindness, humility, gentleness, and patience (Colossians 3:12). Because we're dead to ourselves and hidden with Christ, we never hold grudges or ignore someone we're ︎ated with. In fact, we're quick to forgive other people the ︎v that Jesus forgives us (Colossians 3:13). Most of in love while imitating God (Ephesians 5:1–2).

Love becomes the distinguishing characteristic of being Jesus' follower (John 13:35).

Holiness is a lifestyle that replicates Jesus — the Holy One. Holiness is a lifestyle that's pragmatic and transformational. It touches the marginalized, broken, and lost people of our world. Holiness is blessing an angry waitress with an extraordinary cash tip. Holiness is praying for the sick at Walmart. Holiness is forgiving those you're frustrated with. Holiness is helping people yield their hearts to Jesus. Holiness transforms the atmosphere of the environment you might find yourself in. Holiness will transform a church, city, and region.

Holiness is love in action personifying Christ every moment. It's attractive and far from religion and legalism. Holiness is Christ within, the hope of glory. It's a life possessed by the Holy Spirit and not with lesser things.

Holiness is peace. It's rest. It's victory. It's intimacy. It's not merely being saved from something, namely sin, but for something, and that's Jesus. Holiness is what He does through me, not what I do for Him. It's a lifestyle for everyone because Jesus paid for it. So, let's cash in and become a people of holiness.

PRAYER

Jesus, you did everything possible to make us a holy people. We choose to die to ourselves and become hidden with Christ. Live your life through us. Touch a world and transform people through us in Jesus' name, amen.

APPLICATION

1. Define holiness. List some Scriptures that describe holy people.
2. What are four ways that Scripture describes a holy lifestyle?
3. Would people around you recognize that you have been with Jesus?
4. Are you replicating Christ in all of your actions? Why or why not?

25

Revelation into Revelation

What we listen to will be revealed by what is released from our lives.

In the context of sowing seeds, Jesus made a statement that I've been pondering for months. He had just finished teaching on a parable about a farmer who had dispersed seeds across the ground. The seeds represent the Word of God according to Jesus, and there is no greater truth source than the Word of God (Luke 8:11; John 17:17). The Word is impervious to time, and while grass withers and flowers fade, the Word of God will stand forever (Isaiah 40:8). His Word is so powerful that by the exercise of His will, we were brought forth by its declaration (James 1:21).

It is for reasons such as these that we *must* give our ears to the Word, and nothing else should be allowed to take root in our hearts. Jesus discussed one type of soil as having thorns growing up and choking the Word. What are thorns? In the context of this passage, thorns are evidence that the soil has been exposed to foreign seeds (Luke 8:4–15).

In other words, this indicates that a person has allowed their ears to be subject to things other than the Word of God. In the case of the parable that Jesus told, the fruit of thorns consisted of worries, riches, and pleasures of life. These things choke out the Word and impede the maturity of a Christian.

Other "bad" fruit can spring up when we expose our ears to wrong seeds. Bitterness, jealousy, offense, or unforgiveness, for example, can indicate that we're giving our ears to things other than the Word of God. Our lives will always give evidence of what we're listening to. Jesus said, "Either make the tree good and its fruit good, or make the tree bad and its fruit bad; for the tree is known by its fruit" (Matthew 12:33). What we listen to will be revealed by what is released from our lives. Simply put, bad fruit indicates bad seeds. And the only way bad seeds end up in the soil of our hearts is that we've been negligent concerning what we've allowed to be sown into our spirits.

Jesus went on to say, ". . . For the mouth speaks out of that which fills the heart" (Matthew 12:34b). What you're listening to will eventually be repeated. Take inventory of the words that you've spoken in the last six months. Have they been edifying? Are your words filled with life, or are you repeating gossip or slanderous information about other people?

Keep in mind that this includes the kinds of things you write about concerning other people on Facebook or the Internet. Some believers seem to make it their mission to denigrate those who they disagree with. My question is what are they exposing their ears to that would allow such "thorny" words to proceed from their mouths?

Jesus said, "So take care how you listen; for whoever has, to him *more* shall be given; . . ." (Luke 8:18a). More of what will they be given? The answer is more of what they are listening to. I'm sure that you have heard the phrase "like spirits attract like spirits." If you feast your ears upon rumors and slander, you'll likely be a candidate to receive more of the same. People with this kind of slanderous spirit will find you and fill your heart with seeds of dissension because you've acquired an appetite of listening to those types of things.

On the other hand, if you have been giving your ears to the Word of God, then you've had the privilege to receive revelation. Revelation is a word that means to remove the veil or to expose unseen truth. Paul actually prayed for believers to have a spirit of revelation because they needed their eyes opened to greater truths in the heavenly realms (Ephesians 1:17).

So, when Jesus says that whoever has to him more will be given, He's challenging us to live from revelation to revelation. If we're careful to allow only the right seed to be sown into our hearts, the fruit of our lives will attract the potential of an increased harvest of that very same seed.

Jesus also said that we would have an abundance of what we already have (Matthew 25:29). In the context of these verses, Jesus was referring to our ability to properly steward what has been given to us, and if we do, then there is an increase of the very same thing. In Matthew 25:14-30, Jesus was referring to an increase of resources. In Luke 19:11-27,

He was referring to an increase of responsibility. But in Luke 8:18, the context of these verses points toward listening to the Word of God.

The point is: be careful to what you listen to. Don't expose your ears to harmful seeds; otherwise, your life will be filled with things that could choke or stifle your spiritual progress.

Several years ago, I allowed three bails of straw to sit in my garden for several months, and as a result, I dealt with the fallout of bad seeds for two years later. I tend my garden carefully so as to protect the fruit, and when I do, it enhances the fruit production. Give your ears to the Word of God. Live on the revelation that comes from God's seed planted into your spirit. If you do, then your revelation will lead to an even greater revelation, and you will have an abundance to give away.

PRAYER

Jesus, my ears belong to you. Plant your Word into my heart. With your help, I will not listen to the wrong kind of seed, amen.

APPLICATION

1. Are you holding any bad fruit like unforgiveness, bitterness, anger, or any other ways of the flesh in your heart toward another person? If so, would you be willing to repent, forgive, and even make it right with the person?
2. What kinds of things do you usually allow your ears to listen to?
3. What are some fresh revelations from God's Word that you've received lately?
4. What are some things that continually choke you off from receiving clear revelation? What can be done to change this?

26
Faith and Patience

Believers can actually forfeit their own blessings and fail to inherit what belongs to them by being spiritually lazy and slothful and growing insensitive to the Word of God.

There are two indispensable characteristics necessary for our Christian lives. Before we examine what they are, let's look at what the writer of Hebrews said:

> But, beloved, we are convinced of better things concerning you, and things that accompany salvation, though we are speaking in this way. For God is not unjust so as to forget your work and the love which you have shown toward His name, in having ministered and in still ministering to the saints. And we desire that each one of you show the same diligence

so as to realize the full assurance of hope until the end (Hebrews 6:9–11).

Imagine "better things" that accompany our salvation. What could be greater than freedom from sin and eternal life? The answer is having the favor and blessings of God upon your life now and for generations to come. God swore by His own name to bless and multiply Abraham, and in the context of this passage, we learn that God extends those promises unto us. It's essential for every one of us to remain diligent to the very end. The challenge is *not* to become "sluggish" in our spiritual lives (Hebrews 6:12).

Sluggish (*nothros*) means to become lazy and slothful. It's the same word used in Hebrews 5:11 that speaks about being "dull of hearing." Believers can actually forfeit their own blessings and fail to inherit what belongs to them by being spiritually lazy and slothful and growing insensitive to the Word of God. This is why the writer underscored two characteristics that we're to imitate or two spiritual qualities that all blessed saints in the past possessed. What are these two qualities? They are faith and patience.

Faith and patience were prevalent in every enduring saint in the Bible. Consider Hebrews chapter 11 because it is filled with people who, through faith and patience, were blessed immeasurably by God in spite of what they walked through. Take your pick: by faith Abel, Enoch, Noah, Abraham, Isaac, Joseph, Moses, and Rahab to name a few. Did it take faith and patience for Noah to do what he did? You know the answer to that question. He launched into a project out of obedience to God that brought salvation to his entire household and generations to come. Noah became an heir of righteousness because of faith and patience.

What about Joseph? For over thirteen years, he treasured a dream that God had given to him, and he persevered because of faith and patience. He journeyed from the pit to Potiphar, to prison, and eventually to the palace. He never lost his integrity or his hope in what was promised. Faith and patience in Joseph set up an exodus that rescued over two and half million people after his death.

Then there's Moses, who persevered because he was able to see the unseen (Hebrews 11:27). Faith and patience gave him spiritual eyesight to see what others around him were not able to see.

What is faith? "Now faith is the assurance of *things* hoped for, the conviction of things not seen" (Hebrews 11:1). Assurance means the substance or the foundation upon which someone stands upon. In other words, to say that we have faith actually means that we're standing on something solid.

Conviction carries the idea of something that is seen or proven before it's a reality. It means that one can see something before it's seen. Faith is the eyes to see what others around you may never see. Faith looks beyond the immediate to see the ultimate.

With faith, we look not at what is seen but what is unseen, and that is why we don't lose heart (2 Corinthians 4:16–18). Faith becomes the platform that we stand upon and declare what is yet to come, and nothing or no one will persuade us otherwise. This is why we are to run our spiritual race with endurance and never take our eyes off Jesus (Hebrews 12:1-2). He is the ultimate Victor who, through faith and patience, endured the cross, despising the shame, and sat down at the right hand of the throne of God.

I know people who are standing on the foundation of faith, and they can see their prodigals coming to Christ. They are looking beyond the circumstances that surround their prodigals because they've been captured by another image. They see their prodigals walking in the freedom and power of Christ, so they won't give up or give in because they have faith and patience.

I know people who are standing on the foundation of faith, and they can see their marriage turning around. Despite the fact that circumstances look bleak at the moment, they won't stop pressing in for transformation because they have faith and patience.

I know people who are standing on the foundation of faith, and they can see a specific healing taking place in their bodies. The doctor has reported one thing, but they still believe God's Word concerning the matter, and they won't stop praying because they have faith and patience.

Faith is the ability to see something while patience is the ability to wait and seize it. Faith is saying "yes" to the greater things, and patience is saying "no" to things less than best. Faith is the assurance, and patience is the endurance. Faith is entering the race, and patience is finishing the race. The truth is that faith and patience are indispensable in our Christian walk if we ever hope to see greater things.

There are so many promises in God's Word that accompany our salvation: untold blessings, answers to prayers, miracles, breakthroughs, salvations, revival, and citywide transformation. Those things come to people who aren't sluggish in their spiritual lives but through faith and patience inherit the promises.

Do you have faith and patience?

PRAYER

Jesus, I know there is more. Give me faith and patience to endure to the end and to inherit the promises, amen.

APPLICATION

1. Is your life characterized by faith and patience? Why or why not?
2. List some people in your life who are faith-filled believers. What is the key to their faith?
3. What are some things that you are standing in faith for? Take some time today to ask God for increased faith and patience in your life.

27

The Sword of the Spirit

We can stand firm against the schemes of the enemy by taking up, among other things, a spiritual sword — the sword of the Spirit.

Dressed to Kill, by Rick Renner, is one of the best books on spiritual warfare that I've read. Renner discussed five types of swords that a Roman soldier would have used. The deadliest sword, however, was called a *machaira* sword. In Ephesians 6, the apostle Paul identified seven pieces of armor that we are to use so that we may stand firm against the enemy. Note what he wrote concerning the *machaira* sword in Ephesians 6:17, "And take the helmet of salvation, and the sword of the Spirit, which is the word of God."

The sword (*machaira*) that Paul referenced was approximately nineteen inches long, and both sides of the blade were razor sharp. This sword was used for cutting and slicing flesh. The tip of the sword was turned upward so that it could rip out the entrails of the enemy. It was extremely lethal.

The Sword of the Spirit

Paul said that we could stand firm against the schemes of the enemy by taking up, among other things, a spiritual sword — the sword of the Spirit. The sword of the Spirit is the Word (*rhema*) of God, which is an inspired utterance from the Lord. It can be defined as a spoken word by a living voice or a divine word spoken through the Holy Spirit.

A *rhema* word is a clearly spoken word in undeniable, unmistakable, and unquestionable language that we hear and understand. Renner wrote, "In the New Testament, the word *rhema* carries the idea of a quickened word, such as a word of Scripture or a 'word from the Lord' that the Holy Spirit supernaturally drops into a believer's mind, thus causing it to supernaturally come alive and impart special power or direction to that believer."[5]

Throughout history, there have been men and women who have made critical decisions or life-changing moves simply because they heard a word from the Lord. God spoke an undeniable, unmistakable, and unquestionable word to them, and they obeyed it. As a result, through God's people who were obedient to the spoken Word of God, extraordinary accomplishments have occurred. The sword of the Lord was picked-up by those believers and used to stand firm against the enemy by cutting down the work of darkness.

Much of Paul's ministry was influenced by *rhema* words being spoken to him. For example: God spoke to Paul at the time of his conversion (Acts 9:4–6), God spoke to Ananias concerning Paul's life and need of a healing (Acts 9:10–16), the Holy Spirit spoke at the time of Paul's "commissioning" into public ministry (Acts 13:2), the Holy Spirit warned Paul where he was *not* to preach (Acts 16:6), God spoke to Paul in preparation for a period of persecution that he would experience in Jerusalem (Acts 21:11), and the Holy Spirit spoke concerning Paul's ministry in the city of Rome (Acts 23:11).

We can conclude that Paul used the sword of the Spirit to advance the kingdom of God. He heard the *rhema* Word of God, and by obeying it, the gospel of Christ was advanced against the perils and wiles of the devil. The Holy Spirit desires to speak a *rhema* word to you, too. He wants to speak to you in undeniable, unmistakable, and unquestionable language that you hear and understand. Have you heard a word from the Lord recently?

The challenge becomes living in such a way that we're able to hear the subtle voice of the Holy Spirit. The Bible says today that if we hear His voice, we're not to harden our hearts (Hebrews 4:7). I believe the issue is not if God is speaking but if we're listening.

Recently, I wrote that one of the most significant things we can do to stand firm against the schemes of the enemy is to "listen" to the voice of the Holy Spirit. Life is in His voice. We don't live by bread alone, but by *every* word (*rhema*) that proceeds out of God's mouth (Matthew 4:4). If we live by His words, then, could we spiritually die by the absence of hearing them?

We must arrange our lives in a posture of intimacy to hear what Jesus is saying to us. Choose to live a "Mary lifestyle" at the feet of Jesus. This is a challenge, no doubt, because we live in a "Martha world" that is worried, bothered, and distracted about so many things (Luke 10:38–42). Intimacy with Jesus is fundamental to hearing, and it's how we're equipped to use the sword of the Spirit against the schemes of the enemy.

Additionally, some of the greatest spoken words you will hear occur when you read the written words of God. The Bible says, "All Scripture is inspired by God and profitable for teaching, for reproof, for correction, for training in righteousness; so that the man of God may be adequate, equipped for every good work" (2 Timothy 3:16-17). Become a student of the Bible so that you can be adequately equipped for every work the Lord calls you to do. Read, soak, immerse, listen, study, and memorize the written Word of God, and watch how frequently He will speak a living word into your heart.

Stand firm, my friends, and use the sword of the Spirit against the schemes of the enemy so that you can advance the kingdom of God.

PRAYER

Spirit of the living God, teach me to be a student of the Word. Allow the words to permeate my spirit and to flow out of me. I choose to stand in the strength of Christ against any scheme the enemy can throw at me, amen.

APPLICATION

1. Have you heard the Word (*rhema*) of the Lord lately? If so, describe it. If not, why?
2. The weapon against the enemy is the Word of God. How much of your time daily are you spending preparing yourself for the battlefield?
3. What can you do to increase your ability to better hear the Word?
4. What are some things that you can do to increase your intimacy with Jesus?

28

Life in the Spirit

Life in the Spirit is a day-by-day journey, and there is no limit to what God desires to do through each of us.

I was sitting in an airport waiting for my next flight when I saw a man and his little daughter together. She was about two years old, and she was just learning to walk. Her father held her arms up, and she placed her little feet on top of his feet. Each step that he took, his daughter walked in step with him. She was walking on top of his feet as he balanced her. Watching that made me think about walking in step with the Spirit, and so I want to talk about that in this lesson.

Paul wrote, "Now those who belong to Christ Jesus have crucified the flesh with its passions and desires. If we live by the Spirit, let us also walk by the Spirit" (Galatians 5:24–25). Life in the Spirit will never be possible until we are willing to crucify the flesh. The flesh is contrary to the Spirit, so we will not do the things that please God when flesh remains (Galatians 5:17). There will always be an internal civil war between the flesh and the Spirit until something is done to end the conflict.

There are those who teach that this internal strife is a lifetime struggle—that we must live with this tug-a-war throughout our lives. But the Bible argues differently, we're told to "crucify" the flesh rather than strive against it. When our flesh is executed, it delivers us from the "passions" and "desires" that accompany the flesh. The word passion (*pathema*) is the inclination or propensity of sin. In this context the word means that which befalls us or that which influences us. We will never be able to walk in the Spirit until the influence, the propensity (tendency, leaning, or pull), and the inclination of sin is crucified.

Along with crucifying the flesh with its passions, Paul stated we're to put to death the "desires" of the flesh. Desires (*epithumia*) refer to the longings, cravings, and yearnings of evil doing. Similar to passions, we will never be able to walk freely in the Spirit if these desires are not crucified. Paul said, "Even so consider yourselves to be dead to sin, but alive to God in Christ Jesus" (Romans 6:11).

Thank God that our flesh can be crucified and praise Him that it is possible to die to sin and live freely in Christ. Have you asked God to crucify your flesh? You don't have to strive against the passions and desires of the flesh. You don't have to struggle against the inclinations and longings of sin. You can be free from the duplicity (the battle of two opposing forces) of the Spirit and the flesh (James 4:8).

Our experience with God, however, doesn't stop at merely executing the flesh. Flesh is destroyed so that we can

Life in the Spirit

walk freely in the Spirit. Paul wrote, "If we live by the Spirit, let us also walk by the Spirit" (Galatians 5:25). The word "walk" (*stoicheo*) means to keep in step with someone or to walk in agreement with them. So, we are to walk step-by-step in the Spirit. Think about that: we live and move in Him (Acts 17:28).

If every activity that Jesus did was directed by the Father, then we should expect to walk in the same manner (John 5:19). Everything that we do should be done in the Spirit. Here are just a few examples in the Bible of things that we are to do in the Spirit.

1. We are to learn in the Spirit (John 16:13; 1 John 2:27).
2. We are to witness in the Spirit (Acts 1:8).
3. We are to speak in the Spirit (Acts 2:4; 4:8).
4. We are to follow in the Spirit (Acts 16:6; Romans 8:14).
5. We are to prophesy in the Spirit (Luke 1:67; Acts 2:17).
6. We are to minister in the Spirit (2 Corinthians 3:8).
7. We are to sow in the Spirit (Galatians 6:8).
8. We are to pray in the Spirit (Ephesians 6:18; Jude 20).

The Bible says that we are baptized in the Spirit (Luke 3:16), we are comforted through the Spirit (John 14:16), we are filled with the Spirit (Acts 4:31), and we are cleansed by the Spirit (Acts 15:9). The Holy Spirit empowers (Luke 24:49), teaches (John 14:26), convicts (John 16:8), guides (John 16:13), and reveals (1 Corinthians 2:10).

When we are filled with the Holy Spirit, we will grow nine fruits (Galatians 5:22–23) and be poised to manifest nine functions (1 Corinthians 12:7–10). When we're given the Holy Spirit, He will abide with us and He will be in us

(John 14:17). The Spirit is something that we can ask more of (Luke 11:13), have an unlimited measure of (John 3:34), and always be filled with again and again (Ephesians 5:18, "filled" is a present tense verb). Finally, we were all made to drink of one Spirit (1 Corinthians 12:13), so the Holy Spirit should be the only thing that we quench our thirst with.

Life in the Spirit is a day-by-day journey, and there is no limit to what God desires to do through each of us. But it's essential to keep in step with Him every moment of every day. I have discovered that there are three problems to avoid. First: *walking ahead* of the Spirit because of impetuousness, impatience, and an inability to wait for the Spirit's timing. Sometimes we believe our ideas are going to improve on God's methods, so we step beyond His leadership.

Second: *walking behind* the Spirit because of fear, unbelief, and apathy. Often the problem here is we attempt to reason with the Spirit rather than instantly obey Him; therefore, we're usually a step behind Him.

Third: *walking away* from the Spirit because of negligence, disappointment, or sin. The writer of Hebrews warned us to pay close attention so that we would not drift away (Hebrews 2:1). It is essential to avoid these problems and remain in communion with the Holy Spirit as God designed us to be.

There is no greater joy or no greater possibilities than when we're walking step-by-step in Him. So, allow the Holy Spirit to fill you, cleanse you, consume you, saturate you, deluge you, and lead you. It's a life of joy unspeakable and full of glory.

PRAYER

Holy Spirit of God, fill me daily fresh and new. I desire to live a life walking in your presence day by day. Empower me to flow in the supernatural gifts that you give to me, amen.

APPLICATION

1. How much of your day is spent walking in the fullness of the Spirit?
2. Are you living your life to the full measure of Holy Spirit?
3. Is there anything you need to adapt in to have more of the Spirit in your life?
4. What are some problems that you can avoid in order to stay in step with the Holy Spirit?

29
Being Led by the Spirit

Our lives will always make a difference for God when we live and walk in the Spirit.

Who or what influences your life?

Over my lifetime there have been many people who have influenced my life. Family members, such as my father and grandfather, have shaped the way I think and live. Friends, such as Dan Bohi, Corey Jones, and Kevin Seymour, have deeply influenced my life. One of my spiritual fathers, Ron Frizzell, poured into me in 1997 for almost two years and continues to be an encouragement.

One of my professors, Charles "Chic" Shaver, deeply influenced me, along with two scholars, Jon Mark Ruthven and Gary Greig, who were my doctoral mentors. I've been deeply touched by a revivalist named Randy Clark, who has ministered in more than seventy countries. He prayed an impartation over me in 2008 about redigging the wells in the Holiness movement.

There are people throughout history, such as E. M. Bounds, Maria Woodworth-Etter, Charles G. Finney, Reese Howells, John G. Lake, Aimee Semple McPherson, D. L. Moody, Leonard Ravenhill, and John Wesley, who have lived and modeled God in such a way that it has imprinted my heart.

I could go on—the number is too numerous to count. I honor the anointing that each of these people carries now, and I honor those who diligently walked with God in the past. The body of Christ is filled with many men and woman around the globe who all sing the new song, "Worthy are You to take the book and to break its seals; for You were slain, and purchased for God with Your blood men from every tribe and tongue and people and nation" (Revelation 5:9).

However, in the final analysis, there is no one or nothing that has influenced my life more than the supernatural presence of the Holy Spirit. We are not spiritual orphans abandoned and left alone. Jesus gave us "another Helper, that He may be with (us) forever" (John 14:16b). The Holy Spirit is the promise of the Father (Luke 24:49), and He is a gift to all believers (Acts 2:38). Jesus said the Holy Spirit would "teach you all things" (John 14:26). "All things," Jesus said—imagine that!

John said, "As for you, the anointing which you received from Him abides in you, and you have no need for anyone to teach you; but as His anointing teaches you about all things, and is true and is not a lie, and just as it has taught you, you abide in Him" (1 John 2:27). Talking about being an influence in our lives, who is better than the One who teaches us all things? The greatest teacher, the greatest helper, the greatest comforter, and the greatest influence is the Holy Spirit, and He lives inside you.

The Bible says, "For all who are being led by the Spirit of God, these are sons of God" (Romans 8:14). Being led (*ago*) is a present tense verb that can be translated "constantly influenced." In other words, according to this verse the children of God are those who are constantly being influenced by the Holy Spirit.

Being led by the Spirit is the essence of Ezekiel's prophecy concerning the new covenant. He said of the Lord, "I will put My Spirit within you and cause you to walk in My statutes, and you will be careful to observe My ordinances" (Ezekiel 36:27). The Holy Spirit enables us to walk in righteousness. He actually compels us to live and function in holiness.

The Holy Spirit empowers us to witness, intercedes through our weaknesses, and manifests through us for the profit of all (Acts 1:8; Romans 8:26; 1 Corinthians 12:7). Without the Holy Spirit, we would be left with dead religion because it is the Spirit that gives life (John 6:63; 2 Corinthians 3:6).

I once heard someone say, "Let's all come around the front and spend some time getting into the Spirit." I thought to myself, I don't remember getting *out* of the Spirit. The point is we never have to be absent from His presence. I attempt to steward my life in such a way that I never allow anything to become larger in my mind than my awareness of His manifest presence. I need to do better. What about you?

My deepest desire is to live every moment under the constant influence of the Holy Spirit. This makes life exciting and very adventurous because the Holy Spirit is with me every place that I go, such as Walmart, Starbucks, or Lowes. Moreover, He desires to "get released" from time to time. He should spill out when I bump into people. Graham Cooke once said, "No one is safe around a Spirit-filled believer."

Our lives will always make a difference for God when we live and walk in the Spirit. I'm certain that there have been people in your life who have influenced you in a positive manner. But if not, please take comfort in the fact that you have the abiding, manifest presence of the Holy Spirit who will be "with you and will be in you" as Jesus said (John 14:17b). If you will let Him, the Holy Spirit will become the greatest influence in your life.

PRAYER

God, I thank you for the abiding presence of the Holy Spirit. Baptize me with a fresh touch of your Spirit and influence every move that I make. I pray in Jesus' name, amen.

APPLICATION

1. What are you being led by? The Holy Spirit? Your emotions? The expectation from other people? Your thoughts?
2. Does your life have an on/off switch of living in the Spirit?
3. Using the illustration that Graham Cooke said, "No one is safe around a Spirit-filled believer," are people safe around you? Or are you always looking for opportunities to release the power of the Spirit to people around you?
4. List some people who you have seen walk in the fullness of the Holy Spirit. Contact them, if possible, and ask them to impart that power into your life.

30

Quenching the Spirit

The habit of inserting our will over the subtle promptings of the Spirit on a day-by-day basis fosters insensitivity and callousness to His voice.

Have you ever sensed the Holy Spirit being quenched in a corporate gathering?

Answering that question might be tricky because people feel like various parameters, such as the length of a service, the style of music, or even the type of building you meet in, can quench the Holy Spirit. What does it actually mean to quench the Spirit?

Once I attended a service where several thousand people had gathered. During this service, hundreds, even a thousand or more people, began gathering around the front to seek God, to repent, and to pray. As a result, there was a palpable shift in the atmosphere. The weighty presence of God had moved upon us to the point that it was difficult even to breathe. Most of us were on our faces weeping, broken, and repenting. As I lifted my head, I observed that the leadership of this particular event had joined those seeking God and honoring His presence.

What should you do when that kind of shift happens? My answer is to obey and follow the leadership of God. During that service, the presence of the Lord intensified, and it was obvious that He had an agenda. So, in those moments we should buckle our seatbelts and enjoy the journey. This was more than an emotional moment in the service. In fact, there was no sensationalism occurring, but there was a saturation of brokenness and repentance.

The spiritual outcome naturally was redemption, deliverance, healing, and restoration. The attention and focus were on the presence of God and not any one person leading this event. Like Isaiah experienced when the presence of God came into the temple, most of us were undone (Isaiah 6:1–5). The last thing any one of us wanted to do was to bridle or manage the Holy Spirit. He obviously moved in and manifested Himself on those He loved (John 14:21).

When the Spirit fell on the day of Pentecost, the recipients of that outpouring didn't attempt to control the Spirit. Instead, the Spirit controlled those He fell upon. A few years later, the early church received yet another massive outpouring of the Holy Spirit, and the place where they were meeting was shaken. And yet again they were *all* filled (Acts 4:31). There is no indication that the early church put stipulations upon the Spirit. He fell on His people, and the hungry constituency received Him without reservations.

Quenching the Spirit

Paul wrote, "Do not quench the Spirit" (1 Thessalonians 5:19). The verb quench (*sbennumi*) means to extinguish a fire. It refers to placing a blanket over a flame to suffocate or stifle it. One expositor said this word means to prevent the Holy Spirit from exerting His full influence upon people or on an event. Quenching the Spirit, then, is a willful intention on our part to choose to exert our wills over the will of the Holy Spirit. Quenching the Spirit is often an indicator that people have become accustomed to grieving the Spirit (Ephesians 4:30).

In fact, if we privately grieve the Holy Spirit, we will publicly quench the Holy Spirit. The habit of inserting our will over the subtle promptings of the Spirit on a day-by-day basis fosters insensitivity and callousness to His voice. Over time, we not only become deafened to His tender leadership, but our agendas, good intentions, and well-constructed ministry events will seem more essential in our minds than an apparent interruption from God.

To be honest, those moments when the Holy Spirit redirects a service or pours Himself upon a body of believers can be messy. It requires us to alter our plans or, perhaps, to rewrite our schedules. We may have to "punt" so to speak. Sometimes services will last longer than planned, or an event will extend beyond the allocated dates. Sometimes different songs are sung, and sometimes *no* songs are needed.

The point is that when the Holy Spirit sovereignly decides to interrupt an event or gathering, our responsibility and privilege is to follow Him. We should lean into His agenda and trust His guidance. We should follow His lead and go where He is taking us, and when we do, we will avoid suffocating Him or stifling His influence.

Someone once asked me, "How do you know if the Holy Spirit is sovereignly moving?" Asking that question implies that we've grown distant from His presence. Most of us, if we're intimate with Jesus and walking in the Spirit, will know when He is redirecting an event. This doesn't mean that we avoid planning ministry events, putting together schedules, and organizing service formats. The Holy Spirit can be just as involved in the planning as He can be in the overriding of an event. We should, however, hold all plans loosely. As Pastor Jim Cymbala, Pastor of Brooklyn Tabernacle, once said, "Don't invite the Holy Spirit to come if you're not willing to let Him do what He wants if He does come."

These days I'm learning to live in the abiding presence of the Holy Spirit. But I also desire to be aware of those moments when the Spirit *wrecks* my plans. I love to teach, but if He chooses to speak without my voice, I should be pleased to let that happen. Our worship team prepares every week for an hour of intense worship, but if He chooses to speak without music, we should be pleased to let that happen. I schedule many three- and four-night meetings throughout the year in churches, but if He chooses to move in one night or in seven nights, I should be pleased to follow. It's all about Him and what He desires. I never want to place a blanket over the manifest presence of God.

May we allow His presence to burn hotter and brighter!

PRAYER

Spirit of the living God, we invite you to come into our lives, churches, and events in the way you choose. Our plans are held loosely. We trust you, and we will follow your leadership, amen.

APPLICATION

1. Are there things you do that quench the Spirit of God in your life? What are you going to do to change them?
2. When the Holy Spirit interrupts your plans, how do you typically react?
3. How sensitive are you at a move of the Spirit in a cooperate church service? Can you recognize when something is shifting in the atmosphere around you? During those moments pray that Holy Spirit will have His will and will not be quenched.
4. Are you willing to allow the Holy Spirit to have His way in your life completely?

31

Grieving the Spirit

Don't allow anything into your life that would overshadow your affection for the Spirit.

I have been studying recently about our privilege and responsibility to host the presence of the Holy Spirit. Our entire lives are to be lived and immersed in the Holy Spirit. Paul stated that we actually "live by the Spirit" (Galatians 5:25b). Jesus said, "It is the Spirit who gives life; . . ." (John 6:63a).

We actually don't live spiritually until the Spirit invades and infuses our souls with vitality. Jesus also said of the Spirit, ". . . He abides with you and will be in you" (John 14:17b). Imagine that! The Spirit abides with us. That means He remains, hovers, and tabernacles on and in us. Life should never be boring, right?

Living in the Holy Spirit, however, requires intimacy, obedience, companionship, and most of all, an awareness of Him at all times. If the Holy Spirit is going to remain with

Grieving the Spirit

us, it's imperative that we become sensitive to Him. Life revolves around the Holy Spirit, not us. Think about the riveting question Paul asked in Galatians 3:3 to a group of Christians: "Are you so foolish? Having begun by the Spirit, are you now being perfected by the flesh?" I don't want to treat the Holy Spirit in the same manner as did the Galatian believers who preferred their efforts above the Spirit.

Note this command in Ephesians 4:30 where it says, "Do not grieve the Holy Spirit of God, by whom you were sealed for the day of redemption." Grieve (*lupeo*) means to hurt, abuse, distress, or offend. We can actually *hurt* the Holy Spirit who has been given to us. Do you realize that the Spirit is not merely a force or energy source? He certainly is not an "it." The Holy Spirit is a person. He is the third person of the Trinity. In John chapters 14–16, there are nineteen personal pronouns of "He" or "Him" referring to the Holy Spirit. He really *is* a person. Divine? Yes. Coequal with God? Most certainly true, but He is a person with whom we are to walk in fellowship. With that being said, we are commanded not to grieve Him.

How do we grieve the Holy Spirit? The context of Ephesians 4:25–32 answers that question. We grieve the Holy Spirit the following ways:

1. When we fail to speak the truth to others and give in to inauthenticity or deception (verse 25).
2. When we allow anger to linger and it gives occasion to sin (verse 26).
3. When we give the devil space in our lives or a foothold to influence us (verse 27).

4. When we choose not to work and miss opportunities to generously pour into others with resources (verse 28).
5. When we use our mouth to destroy people with barren, lifeless words and fail to edify and impart grace with our tongues (verse 29).
6. When we allow offenses to fester and poison our attitudes, speech, and behavior (verse 31).
7. When we don't forgive others the same way Christ forgave us (verse 32).

Any of these practices are offensive and hurtful to the Holy Spirit. Moreover, the only way we could ever participate in those grieving activities is by resisting and rejecting the ongoing promptings of the Holy Spirit. He came, Jesus said, to guide us into all truth (John 16:13). Therefore, we actually grieve the Spirit—who is called the Spirit of truth—by suppressing Him, a practice—I might add—that incurs the wrath of God (Romans 1:18).

The Holy Spirit can also be grieved by our thoughts, motives, and intentions. The Pharisees honored God with their lips, but their hearts were far from Him (Mark 7:6). The Holy Spirit functions beyond merely guiding our behavior. He looks inward and is very aware of attitudes that initially may not be observant to other people. He looks into our hearts and can see bigotry, arrogance, lust, anxiety, fear, or distractions.

Jesus looked at Martha and perceived that she was "worried and bothered" about many things, in spite of the fact

Grieving the Spirit

that she was in the midst of ministry (Luke 10:41). On the outside, she appeared to be productive, but on the inside, she was in trouble. The Holy Spirit is always aware of the state of our hearts. While that fact may bring conviction to some, to others it is a comfort. There is no one who knows you better than the Holy Spirit. He is *your* Comforter (John 14:16).

My encouragement to you is to live consciously aware of His presence and activity in your day-to-day lifestyle. Don't allow anything into your life that would overshadow your affection for the Spirit. Remember, the most important thing you will do is the next thing that He prompts you to do. Obey His guidance swiftly and promptly.

Quiet your heart often in His presence and invite Him to speak. Learn to say only what He says. Pray what He gives you and give away what He's doing. And if, during the speaking of His still small voice, you discover that you've grieved Him, then fall before the Holy Spirit in repentance. Brokenness and repentance creates the posture that's most attractive to the habitation of the Holy Spirit.

PRAYER

Dear God, teach us to walk by your Holy Spirit. Give us a greater sensitivity to the gentle ways in which you speak, guide, and move in our lives. Let us know if we have grieved you, amen.

APPLICATION

1. How is grieving the Holy Spirit different than quenching the Holy Spirit?
2. Is there something that the Holy Spirit is showing you that grieves Him about your life? Repentance is the best response to grieving the Holy Spirit.
3. When we think more highly of ourselves than others, we grieve the Holy Spirit. Think of ways to honor others this week over yourself and watch what happens both in their lives and in your life.

32

Dove or Pigeon

I don't believe Jesus walked around with an actual bird on His shoulder, but I'm certain that the Holy Spirit remained with Him.

Have you looked at your shoulder lately?

John the Baptist was sent to baptize in water, and he also was to look for the coming one who would baptize with the Holy Spirit. John was told that the Holy Spirit would descend upon Jesus and "remain" upon Him, and this would distinguish Jesus as the Messiah (John 1:33).

Sure enough, "John testified saying, 'I have seen the Spirit descending as a dove out of heaven, and He remained upon Him'" (John 1:32). I don't believe Jesus walked around with an actual bird on His shoulder, but I'm certain that the Holy Spirit remained with Him. Remain (*meno*) means to dwell, sojourn with, abide, and tabernacle upon. The Holy Spirit, the dove, never departed from Jesus, which tells us that He lived and adjusted His life, in every manner, to host the Holy Spirit.

Years ago, my wife and I owned a talking parakeet. He would sit on our shoulders chirping and saying various words that we had taught him. Although he was frequently out of the cage, he was never out of the house. We feared that he would fly away, so we always kept him in the house — usually on our shoulders.

One day Cindy and I were having a cookout, and while I was preparing the grill, Cindy came outside with the tray of hamburgers. I looked up and spotted our parakeet on her shoulder. Quickly, when I alerted her to the parakeet's presence, she carefully sat down the tray of meat and proceeded to walk back into the house carefully, making no sudden moves. Every move that she made was accomplished with our bird in mind. Her awareness of the bird required an adjustment in how she walked.

How would you walk if you lived consciously aware of the dove, the Holy Spirit, resting on your shoulder? Would you adjust your conversations, temperament, choices, or character?

I learned recently that a dove and a pigeon are from the same family, yet they are worlds apart in their characteristics. Largely, pigeons can tolerate noise, recklessness, and many distractions. They are a boisterous, feisty bird that will easily adjust to almost anyone. Not so with a dove, they are much more temperamental. Noise, distractions, and sudden moves easily frighten doves away.

Dove or Pigeon

If you want a pigeon to remain, you can basically go about your life as normal because it will adjust to you. If, however, you desire to have a dove remain, then you have to mindfully adjust your lifestyle to its temperament. Jesus experienced three years of ministry and many trials, persecutions, and eventually execution, and yet He never startled the dove from His shoulder. Everything Jesus said and did was accomplished with the Spirit in mind. Jesus altered His life around the sacred habitation of the Holy Spirit. The dove remained with Jesus, and if Jesus lived with the constant presence of the Spirit, then we're called to do the same.

Admittedly, too many of us have hosted a pigeon and thought it was the dove. Our reckless, insensitive lifestyles have long startled away the dove and left us with a flock of pigeons. When Paul identified the deeds of the flesh in Galatians, he was describing people who thought little of the dove—the Holy Spirit. "Now the deeds of the flesh are evident, which are: immorality, impurity, sensuality, idolatry, sorcery, enmities, strife, jealousy, outburst of anger, disputes, dissensions, factions, envying, drunkenness, carousing, and things like these . . ." (Galatians 5:19–21a).

These kinds of characteristics may not startle arrogant pigeons, but the dove—Holy Spirit—has nothing to do with that kind of behavior. In fact, a person who participates in such things "will not inherit the kingdom of God" (Galatians 5:22b). I wonder how many churches have quenched the Spirit and settled for pigeon religion.

I've been to churches where it felt as if they had "trained" the bird to move on command. In reality, they had a form of godliness but denied its power (2 Timothy 3:5). Pigeon religion will despise prophetic utterances (1 Thessalonians 5:20) and squeeze out the manifestations of the Spirit (1 Corinthians 12:7). If we allow pigeons to remain, we will "grieve the Holy Spirit of God" (Ephesians 4:30) with bitterness, wrath, anger, clamor, slander, malice, and unforgiveness (Ephesians 4:31–32).

Paul wrote, "But I say, walk by the Spirit, and you will not carry out the desire of the flesh" (Galatians 5:16). Consider this: if you walk hosting the dove, you will not allow a pigeon to roost. What is the evidence that you are walking with a dove, the Holy Spirit, abiding with you? The Bible says your life will manifest "love, joy, peace, patience, kindness, goodness, faithfulness, gentleness, [and] self-control" (Galatians 5:22–23).

If you're walking with the dove, then your prayer life will be effective because you'll pray in the Spirit (Ephesians 6:18; Jude 20). If you're walking with the dove, then you won't lose heart doing good because you know that sowing to the Spirit will reap eternal life (Galatians 6:8–9). If you're walking with the dove, then the Spirit will be manifested for the common good of those around you (1 Corinthians 12:7).

If you're walking with the dove, then your life will release freedom in the Spirit to those in bondage (2 Corinthians 3:17). If you're walking with the dove, then the Spirit will teach you all things and remind you what Jesus said (John 14:26). If you're walking with the dove, then the Spirit will guide you into all truth (John 16:13). Truly, if you're walking with the dove, then you'll be more like Jesus every day.

Dove or Pigeon

My challenge is to live consciously aware of the Holy Spirit every moment of our lives. Let's not allow anything around us to become larger in our minds than the Holy Spirit who is upon us. Consider how each conversation and every action can, and should, be shaped with the dove in mind.

May the dove (Holy Spirit) remain with us!

PRAYER

Jesus, show me what I have resting on me? Is it a dove or pigeon? Make me more aware of your Spirit. I'm asking that your Holy Spirit remains on me every day of my life, amen.

APPLICATION

1. What are you hosting on your shoulder, a pigeon or a dove? Do the words you speak to family, friends, or co-workers scare off the dove?
2. What are some reactions that typically show a pigeon mentality in your life? What actions demonstrate a dove lifestyle?
3. How would your lifestyle need to change if you consistently host the presence of the Holy Spirit?

33

Unaware of His Presence

Allowing our eyes to be diverted from Christ puts us at risk of moving outside of His presence.

There's a particular passage in Luke that has challenged me on several levels. It states:

> Now His parents went to Jerusalem every year at the Feast of the Passover. And when He became twelve, they went up *there* according to the custom of the Feast; and as they were returning, after spending the full number of days, the boy Jesus stayed behind in Jerusalem. But His parents were unaware of it, but supposed Him to be in the caravan, and went a day's journey; and they *began* looking for Him among their relatives and acquaintances. When they did not find Him, they returned to Jerusalem looking for Him. Then, after three

days they found Him in the temple, sitting in
the midst of the teachers, both listening to them
and asking them questions (Luke 2:41–46).

The earthly parents of the Messiah left Jerusalem without Jesus in their midst, and they were totally unaware. How could this have happened? The word "unaware" implies a lack of intimate knowledge. It tells us that somewhere along the line Mary and Joseph took their eyes off of Jesus and placed their attention on something other than Him. Have you ever taken your eyes off of Jesus? The writer of Hebrews emphatically states, "Fixing our eyes on Jesus, the author and perfecter of faith, . . ." (Hebrews 12:2a). Allowing our eyes to be diverted from Christ puts us at risk of moving outside of His presence.

I realize that some people may respond that Jesus will never leave us, yet I'm referring to the manifest presence of Jesus in our lives. While His omnipresence is everywhere, the supernatural anointing of His manifest presence can lift from a believer, a church, or a pastor. Using this story in Luke as an illustration, we can continue in our activities unaware that the anointing, His manifest presence, is no longer with us.

Returning to the question, how could Mary and Joseph leave without Jesus in their midst? My answer is familiarity. Familiarity can breed a spiritual paradigm that makes us comfortable with the patterns of Jesus that, if we're not careful, diminish anticipation for anything "out of the ordinary" from Him.

Think about this: Mary and Joseph journeyed to Jerusalem for twelve years to celebrate the Feast of the Passover. For twelve years, Jesus went with and returned with them. This became their paradigm. This became their "custom" (Luke 2:43). What they did year after year became a spiritual pattern, and after twelve years of doing the same thing, they didn't anticipate that Jesus would do anything different.

I wonder if we are any different. Have we become so comfortable with our Sunday gatherings that we don't anticipate Jesus doing something different? What about our revivals, camp meetings, or conferences? Sometimes a familiarity with these kinds of events can overshadow our expectations that Jesus might move in a completely different manner.

Most revivals of the past have ended because the recipients of the original move of God became accustomed to how the Spirit moved. So, when the Spirit moved in a different manner, they rejected the Spirit's outpouring. I'm broken by how many churches simply "journey on" in the absence of His presence, yet they fulfill their customs of familiarity.

Jesus remained behind in Jerusalem on this particular occasion, and Mary and Joseph missed the "new move" of the Spirit. Their lack of awareness led them to make a spiritual assumption: they "supposed Him to be in the caravan" (Luke 2:44). I don't want to make spiritual assumptions because they are proof of a lack of intimacy and the height of spiritual arrogance.

Samson made the spiritual assumption that he could break free from fetters as in other times, and the assumption cost him his eyes (Judges 16:20). King Saul made a spiritual assumption that he should make an unlawful sacrifice and he lost his anointing (1 Samuel 15:26). We cannot effectively serve God by "supposing" that His manifest presence is with us. We must live with our ears inclined toward the Lord because life is in His voice (Isaiah 55:3). Let's learn to move *only* at His impulse. Jesus modeled for us a life that was led—every moment watching the Father (John 5:19). Let's live the same way.

Mary and Joseph searched for Jesus among their relatives and acquaintances but to no avail. They retraced their steps, and their search led them back to the temple, where they found Him. That is a good reminder for us. Jesus told a busy church to return to their first love (Revelation 2:4). If you've not sensed His manifest presence in your life, return to the place where you "lost" His weighty presence. I would suggest that we return in brokenness and repentance and fall in love with Him once again.

This story in Luke is a reminder of living in intimacy. It speaks to me about knowing and living in the Father's business. In fact, His business is much more important than my business. This story challenges me to adjust my life to Jesus rather than the other way around. It convicts me about my tendency of placing a paradigm above the sovereign moves of the Spirit.

I must remain a novice when it comes to Jesus and the way He chooses to move. I don't want to assume anything. Years ago, we use to sing a song that said, "Every move I make, I make in Him."[6] I want that to be true in your life and mine. I want to walk in step with Jesus every moment of every day. It certainly is possible (Galatian. 5:25).

Let's not let a day go by where we are unaware of His presence.

PRAYER

Jesus, if I'm moving ahead of you, please let me know, and if I'm lagging behind, please convict my heart. I don't want to live unaware of your presence in my life. Help me to remain at your feet, amen.

APPLICATION

1. How could have Mary and Joseph left without Jesus?
2. Have you ever made spiritual assumptions? If so, how?
3. How can you become more sensitive to the presence of Christ in your life?
4. What new ways do you believe the Holy Spirit is desiring to move in your life?

34

Leaders or Followers

The greatest leader is a follower. The greatest need of the hour in our churches is for men and women to move only at the impulse of Jesus.

My friend Hal Perkins spent a few days ministering to our church. His influence has left a tremendous impact, not only upon our congregation but also in my personal life. Hal challenged us by saying that the church doesn't need as many leaders as it does followers. We need less people standing before our churches and declaring, "I think," "I feel," or "I want." Hal's response to those kinds of statements is humorous but convicting: "Who cares?" The *real* question is: what does Jesus say?

The greatest leader is a follower. The greatest need of the hour in our churches is for men and women to move *only* at the impulse of Jesus. If you think about it, Jesus lived as a follower and, therefore, is our greatest Leader. "Therefore,

Jesus answered and was saying to them, 'Truly, truly, I say to you, the Son can do nothing of Himself, unless it is something He sees the Father doing; for whatever the Father does, these things the Son also does in like manner'" (John 5:19).

Followers remain in a posture of intimacy with Jesus and, therefore, their every thought, decision, and move is guided by His manifest presence (John 16:13). Followers can say, "In Him we live and move and exist" (Acts 17:28). Followers don't make spiritual assumptions. They don't allow emotions or feelings to dictate their actions. They don't minister out of "good ideas," rather they minister out of "God ideas."

Followers don't need a consensus to do what is right because they aren't looking to people for affirmation; instead, they keep their eyes on Jesus who perfects their faith (Hebrews 12:2). Jesus didn't even speak His own words. He only spoke and said what the Father told Him (John 12:50). What if you only spoke when the Father gave you something to say? Probably more of our words would be filled with the Spirit and not with the flesh.

The early believers, churches, and ministries were established not by great leaders but by great followers. The prophets and teachers were all together in Antioch "ministering" to the Lord (Acts 13:2). It doesn't say that they were strategizing. They weren't sitting around tables designing ministry slogans and alliterated mission plans. They weren't talking about better programs that they could pull off. What were they doing? They were fasting together and seeking the presence of the Lord. They were focused on the manifest presence of Jesus. They were actually being followers, not leaders.

In that kind of atmosphere, the Holy Spirit spoke with specific instructions. Inspiration came from heaven and not from earth, and Barnabas and Saul (Paul) were chosen and sent out by the Holy Spirit (Acts 13:2-4). When decisions were made in the early church, they did what "seemed good to the Holy Spirit" first, and then they made their decisions (Acts 15:28). The Holy Spirit forbid them to speak the Word in Asia during one of their ministry trips and led them away from another city (Acts 16:7-6). By being a sensitive follower, Paul was led to Philippi, a leading city of Macedonia, and a church was started there (Acts 16:12-13). My point is, like Jesus, the early Christians were followers of the Holy Spirit, and great followers make great leaders.

In Luke chapter four, I've observed three things concerning Jesus: First, Jesus was full of the Holy Spirit. Second, He was led of the Spirit. Third, He functioned in the power of the Spirit. Perhaps the church has become content with simply being full of the Spirit, but we aren't being led—moment by moment—by the Spirit. Therefore, we aren't functioning in the power of the Spirit.

Jesus said that we would replicate His works and do even greater things (John 14:12), but my honest observation is that I'm not seeing a lot of extraordinary power in churches. To be *very* candid, I'm not doing everything Jesus did—yet. He said that I was to be exactly like Him (Luke 6:40). John said that I was to walk "in the same manner as He walked" (1 John 2:6). I don't believe the problem is on His end!

Perhaps then, the problem is that we have jumped from desiring to being filled with the Holy Spirit to simply desiring His power, and the missing link is being led. Because Jesus was led, He was taken through the wilderness, persecution, rejection, betrayal, and eventually to a cross. He never stopped being led and, in fact, every moment of His life was shaped and fashioned by the impulse of the Spirit. As a result, He functioned with amazing power.

We've all been commissioned to preach the gospel, heal the sick, cleanse the lepers, cast out demons, and even raise the dead (Matthew 10:7-8). Additionally, we've all been commissioned to raise-up followers (disciples) who will replicate Jesus (Matthew 28:19-20). But I don't believe that we will fulfill the commission accounts with only better leadership strategies. I believe that we will do what Jesus did, and even greater, when we become better followers.

We must remain in a posture of intimacy with Jesus. We must remain seated with Christ in heavenly places (Ephesians 2:6). He's inside each of us, so every thought must be taken captive and brought to Him until we have the mind of Christ (2 Corinthians 10:5; 1 Corinthians 2:16). We must learn to be led moment by moment throughout our days, following every impulse and direction of the Holy Spirit. And if we're filled with the Holy Spirit and being led by the Spirit, we'll most certainly minister in the power of the Spirit.

Become a better leader by being a better follower.

PRAYER

Lead me, guide me, and speak to me. My life belongs to you, Jesus. My desire is to be a better follower of you. Possess me and live through me every moment of my days, amen.

APPLICATION

1. Are you following the greatest Leader of all time, Jesus, or are you following your own impulses and good ideas?
2. What would your life look like if you only did exactly what Jesus led you to do?
3. What hinders you from hearing and obeying His leadership?
4. Describe an example of being led by Jesus.

35

Revival Is Messy

To seek a revival is to desire seeing your entire city overrun by the manifest presence of God. True revival will start to affect the climate around your church.

All across our nation I hear the same plea over and over again, "We want revival." Churches sing about it, pray about it, and preach about it. I was in a church once that said they wanted revival regardless of the cost. While I'm in agreement with the desires of so many people about revival, I'm not sure that we really understand what a *true* revival would do.

To start with, revival by its very definition implies that we are dead. So, our immediate desire for revival should extend well beyond filling empty seats in our churches with new prospects; rather, it should be to resuscitate our dead, dry, and barren wastelands. If we're going to request revival, we must first repent for abdicating our position of authority with Christ for the works of the flesh.

To be honest, we wouldn't need revival if we truly remained in the Spirit. The prophet Jeremiah stated that God's people had forsaken Him and hewed cisterns that didn't hold water (Jeremiah 2:13). That statement identifies the peril of churches across America today and explains why we actually need revival.

Revival will also disturb the status quo. Before Jesus established Himself as the "Lord of the temple," He overturned tables and benches, and He drove out various merchants (Matthew 21:12). In other words, the activity within the temple was reformed. When Jesus revives your church, certain ministries may be overturned and driven out. Chances are you will not continue doing what you did before if Jesus brings revival.

In Acts 2:1, the Holy Spirit fell like a violent rushing wind, causing believers to speak with such utterances that people thought they were drunk. In Acts 4:31, the Holy Spirit caused the place where the church had assembled to be shaken. In Acts 9:4, the Holy Spirit caused a man to fall to the ground and become blind for several days. In Acts 16:26, the Holy Spirit caused a great earthquake and shook the foundations of a prison house. I have discovered that the Holy Spirit is good, but He's not safe. When the reviving power of the Holy Spirit comes upon a church, generally everything that we do will be shaken and disturbed.

What I've often discovered is that people desire revival until it actually shows up. Their present wineskin doesn't allow for the fresh outpouring of "new wine" because they have become accustomed to a form of godliness with no power (Luke 5:37; 2 Timothy 3:5). When the Holy Spirit manifests in extraordinary ways, they take issue with what they observe to be "strange fire."

I've heard the story many times about a pastor or small a group of people who fasted and prayed for a fresh outpouring of God's Holy Spirit. When God answered that prayer, a few folks resisted the new move of God because He came in ways they least expected. The outpourings of God's Holy Spirit rarely fall in repeated manners.

The tragedy is that many people have become so unfamiliar with His actual presence that they can't discern when He settles into a room and moves upon people. Becoming insensitive to the workings of the Holy Spirit is a dangerous place to be. The religious leaders of Jesus' day were accused of blasphemy because they mistook His manifestations for the work of Satan (Matthew 12:22-32).

Consider also that revival will expose all sin and call all flesh to be crucified. Nothing is hidden when the presence of the Holy Spirit settles upon us. The light of God's glory brings conviction to everyone who is unclean. Isaiah couldn't flee when the presence of God moved into the temple: he was found out. He was undone and sorely in need of cleansing (Isaiah 6:1-7).

Unless we are willing to die a deeper death and seek a deeper cleansing, revival will be very uncomfortable. At the start of this year, I was in a service where the manifest presence of God came like a search light. Areas of my heart were exposed that I was not able to see before. I soon found myself confessing those things and allowing the Holy Spirit to purge my heart.

Revival often gathers the prodigals and refurbishes our passion to reach the lost as well. So when "sinners" come into the church with their array of issues, it can make for interesting moments. Like Bartimaeus shouting when Jesus walked by, sometimes new believers don't know how to behave in church. They need to be instructed and taught with love and grace.

Additionally, if we are truly reaching the lost, then there will be those entering our churches who are demonically oppressed. We experienced someone demonically manifesting during our altar call. We silenced the evil presence and cast it out. What I'm saying is revival can be messy. Proverbs 14:4 says, "Where no oxen are, the manger is clean, But much revenue *comes* by the strength of the ox." If we want the blessing of having an ox in our stall, then we will have to deal with messes now and then. I would rather tolerate the mess of revival than to be clean out of business.

Finally, revival involves more than reformation of our local church. True revival will include citywide transformation. To seek a revival is to desire seeing your entire city overrun by the manifest presence of God. True revival will start to affect the climate around your church. It will affect the way we pray for our city and how we treat people within our community. We will start to speak blessings over our city, believing that one day it will be exalted (Proverbs 11:11).

By now you realize that revival is so much more than having special services during the week. It's much more than praying and fasting for a week or two before the services or inviting a coworker or neighbor to the meetings. That may be a start, but let's not stop there. Let's press in for a mighty outpouring of God's Holy Spirit—a revival God's way, which causes a ripple effect that will touch nations.

This much for sure: true revival is worth whatever mess it might cause.

PRAYER

Revive me, Oh Lord, not for a moment or a day but for a lifetime. May I live for revival regardless of the mess it might cause, amen.

APPLICATION

1. What is the cost you willing to pay for revival in your family, church, and city?
2. Is there something that you need to lay down to see a great outpouring of revival?
3. Have you ever experienced a true revival? If so, explain.
4. Form a group of people who will pray and press in together weekly for an outpouring of the Holy Spirit so that your city will experience a city-wide, transforming revival.

36

Academics Versus Anointing

Learn all that you can by going to school, college, or graduate school. But please, in the midst of your educational process, avail yourself to the presence and power of the Holy Spirit.

What qualifies you for ministry?

I was having a conversation recently with someone about the vanity and superficiality of placing too much confidence in our education. The truth is many young ministers have experienced an erosion of their faith because they entered college or Bible school and were insulted for actually believing the Bible. Too many educators have elevated their opinions over the truths of God's Word.

Worse still, some of the fundamental assignments that Jesus commissioned His "students" to fulfill are being abolished through "higher reasoning." Think about it: our Christian educational process awards diplomas to students who enter into churches with little or no knowledge about the supernatural power of the Holy Spirit (Matthew 10:7–8). What I find even more disheartening is that these extraordinary activities are often denigrated in the "educated" mind.

We have elevated academics over the anointing in preference of promoting someone to a prominent position of leadership based on the degrees behind their name or from the accolades in the wake of their success. It's a good thing that we weren't electing the positions in the New Testament church because we would have missed the characteristics they looked for. The early church looked for people with a good reputation and those filled with the Holy Spirit and with wisdom (Acts 6:3). Two of the lay leaders chosen, Stephen and Philip, operated in power, wonders, signs, and miracles (Acts 6:8; 8:6–7).

Why wouldn't we consider those same qualifications for someone to lead a church or to sit on a board? What if we honored the anointing more than anything else? I don't negate the need for people to be fully trained in a Bible college or seminary. I have spent many hours, and many dollars, pursuing a formal education. Moreover, I have had several professors over the years who have mentored me in the things of the Spirit, for which I'm grateful. Yet, I heard some things that grieved my spirit.

It's interesting to note that 65 percent of the words in the gospel of Mark describing Jesus' public ministry were about supernatural acts of power. Yet sometimes the educational process in our Christian colleges and seminaries rarely addresses the supernatural activities of Jesus or how they might be practiced in our daily lives.

Academics Versus Anointing

If that is correct, then what are students being prepared to do? I certainly have no problem with teaching young people the myriad of subjects in their Christian education, but where are the classes about speaking prophetically over our cities? Where are the classes about intercessory prayer, desperation for the presence of God, fasting, healing, and crying out for fresh encounters with God? Where are the classes that study the supernatural gifts in 1 Corinthians 12 that should manifest through Spirit-filled believers?

People will push back and tell me that we can have both academics *and* anointing. I certainly agree, but the scales have been tipped for many generations in favor of one's educational status at the expense of the power of the Holy Spirit. Paul said, "Let no man deceive himself. If any man among you thinks that he is wise in this age, he must become foolish, so that he may become wise. For the wisdom of this world is foolishness before God. . . ." (1 Corinthians 3:18–19a).

When Paul first came to Corinth, he chose to surrender his academic resume in favor of the anointing of the Spirit. He was educated at the feet of Gamaliel (Acts 22:3), a Hebrew of Hebrews who was blameless concerning the Law as a Pharisee (Philippians 3:5–6). This educated man determined to know nothing among the Corinthians "except Jesus Christ, and Him crucified" (1 Corinthians 2:3). His message was not a well-crafted, polished speech but one that was delivered in the "demonstration of the Spirit and of power" (1 Corinthians 2:5).

Paul later wrote, ". . . The Lord knows the reasonings of the wise, that they are useless" (1 Corinthians 3:20b).

Reasonings (*dialogismos*) refer to deliberating, arguing, and debating. This reasoning comes merely from the mind or what a person may think about or even have knowledge of. This kind of reasoning is useless (*mataios*), which means empty, fruitless, and powerless. The operation of the mind without the presence and power of the Spirit is foolishness, and it lacks the ability to bring transformation in people's lives. This verse describes someone who places his or her mind over the Spirit. What we know can never trump *who* we know; namely, Jesus Christ.

What is the point of this lesson? In the words of Leonard Ravenhill, "With all your getting, get unction." Learn all that you can by going to school, college, or graduate school. But please, in the midst of your educational process, avail yourself to the presence and power of the Holy Spirit.

Moreover, if you've never had the opportunity to obtain a formal education, please do not feel insecure around educated people. Never hang your head in shame because Jesus is the One who qualifies you. He told His students that their preparation for ministry would come when they were "clothed with power from on high" (Luke 24:49). Pray for wisdom because you will receive it generously (James 1:5), seek the revelation of the Lord (Ephesians 1:17), immerse yourself in God's Word so that you'll be quipped for every good work (2 Timothy 3:17) and abide moment by moment in the presence of the Holy Spirit (Galatians 5:25).

Think about this: the same Spirit who raised Jesus from the dead "dwells in you" (Romans 8:11). You're qualified for any task the Spirit leads you to. His power inside you will

Academics Versus Anointing

do "far more abundantly beyond all that [you] ask or think" (Ephesians 3:20).

Anointed with the Spirit is good, anointed with the Spirit *and* academics is good, but without His extraordinary, supernatural presence operative in our lives, we lack much—no matter how many degrees are behind our names.

PRAYER

Jesus, I'm grateful for the opportunities that you gave me to learn, but in the process please never let me forget that your Holy Spirit is my greatest Teacher. Your Word and Spirit qualify me for ministry, amen.

APPLICATION

1. What has been your greatest source of education over the last year?
2. Do you ever compare yourself to others who have more education, more experience in the church, or even a longer walk with Christ? Why or why not?
3. Is the passion to study the Word of God and flow with the Holy Spirit as strong as it was when you first became a Christian? If not, what has changed your motivation?
4. Are you flowing in the supernatural power of the Holy Spirit? How or why not?
5. What are some things that the Holy Spirit has recently taught you?

37

A Prophetic Lifestyle

Whatever God asks next of you, obedience to that prompting is the greatest thing that you will do at that moment.

Dan Bohi often asks, "What is the most important thing that you'll ever do?" We'll answer that question in a moment.

Jesus and His disciples had entered Samaria. The disciples had gone into the city to buy food while Jesus remained relaxing by a well. A woman from the city came to draw water and Jesus said, "Give me a drink" (John 4:7). No doubt His request was met with a bit of surprise because in that culture Jews didn't interact with Samaritans. Jesus, however, was operating within the rules of a different culture. He was functioning out of the kingdom of Heaven. In fact, Jesus taught us to pray, "Your kingdom come" (Matthew 6:10). It was His desire that all followers would make every move from heaven to earth. Let that thought sink in for a moment.

When you live from heaven to earth, you carry a kingdom mindset with you everywhere you go, and there are no limitations when you function from that perspective. The possibilities are endless because the kingdom is at hand (Matthew 4:17). Living from heaven to earth is the posture of being seated in heavenly realms as Paul described in Ephesians 2:6. Therefore, in this posture you move only on heaven's impulse.

There is no such thing as a "random" act of kindness. Every act is to be prompted by the direction of the Father. Jesus said that He could do nothing of Himself but only what He saw the Father doing (John 5:19). So, what is the most important thing you will ever do? Dan answers: "The next thing the Spirit asks you to do!" It might be to buy someone's lunch, to tip the waiter a sizable amount, to pray healing over someone at a shopping mall, or to share your faith with your neighbor. Whatever God asks next of you, obedience to that prompting is the greatest thing that you will do at that moment.

I believe that when Jesus was resting by the well, the Father said to Him, "Ask her for a drink of water and watch what I will do." Heaven was invading earth at that moment, and this precious woman was about to be introduced to the living water. Pay attention to these kinds of leadings when you are out in public. Don't minimize them in your mind or talk yourself out of obedience because of fear.

While I was getting ready to board a plane, I saw a man with a veteran's hat on. I felt prompted by the Spirit to thank him for his service to our country, and when I did, he choked up and told me about receiving Christ while in the navy. I knelt beside him and his wife, and I prayed health and blessings over them.

While at a restaurant during a layover that same day, I felt led to give the waiter a $20 tip, and then I told him about Jesus. On another flight I prophesied over a woman beside me and prayed that God would heal her ear. A few days ago, I was coming out of the library in our town, and I saw two guys standing outside smoking. The Holy Spirit prompted me to ask them how I could bless them. They both told me about a few things that were going on in their lives, so I told them about Jesus, prayed blessings over them, and then bought their lunches.

These are examples of the kingdom of God reaching into earth. They are moments when the heavenly realm invades the earthly realm, and God desires to use you and me in that process. No action is insignificant when we're responding in obedience to the heavenly voice.

Paul wrote, "Pursue love, yet desire earnestly spiritual *gifts*, but especially that you may prophesy" (1 Corinthians 14:1). It starts with love. Why do we minister to people? Why do we reach out to others? Why do we desire to be used by God to touch a world? It's because of love, and if we're truly in Christ, then we're on a journey of pursuing love every day. Love never fails (1 Corinthians 13:8), so you can't screw up if your motive is love.

Paul then said to desire the spiritual (*pneumatikos*), which is a word for the supernatural. It refers to the Holy Spirit blowing through your life and influencing you. Who wouldn't desire that kind of experience? We should all be zealous for those moments when the Spirit flows through us and touches a needy person standing in front of us.

Finally, Paul said "especially that you may prophesy." The simplest definition of prophesying is speaking to others what the Spirit is speaking to you. When you prophesy, you're simply the mouthpiece of God speaking His words of life, hope, and healing to others.

I'm talking about a prophetic lifestyle, where every moment we're living with our ears bent toward heaven ready to release upon others life-giving words and actions given to us by the Holy Spirit. Sometimes it will start with the simplest conversations with people like Jesus did, such as, "Give me a drink!" And the next thing that might happen is an entire city will come to believe in Jesus because you spoke prophetically into someone.

Be ready because after the next thing that He asks of you, and He will ask, something amazing will be about to happen. A kingdom invasion is about to take place, and you're the instrument God desires to use.

PRAYER

Spirit of the living God, I'm all yours. Remove fear, doubt, and insecurity from me, and fill me with your Spirit and with boldness. Speak to me so I can speak to others. I'm ready to live prophetically for you, in Jesus' name, amen.

APPLICATION

1. Are you ready and willing to do the next thing that God is asking you to do, even if it's way out of your comfort zone? Why or why not?
2. Are you ever hindered to do what Jesus tells you? Why or why not?
3. Does your life reflect 1 Corinthians 14:1? Are you truly pursing love? Do you desire to be influenced by the Spirit? Are you speaking prophetically?
4. Begin journaling all the small promptings of the Lord as you act upon them, and over time watch how the Lord will entrust more and more to you.

38

Greater Manifestations of the Spirit

You are to be an instrument that God uses to constantly display the work of the Holy Spirit.

The apostle Paul wrote, "But to each one is given the manifestation of the Spirit for the common good" (1 Corinthians 12:7). To each person, Paul said. No one is left out of this blessing. If you are Spirit-filled, then this includes you. To every one of us is "given" (*didomi*). This is a present tense verb that states something being bestowed or imparted without stopping. In other words, there is no end to the impartation that is given to us.

What is imparted? Paul said the manifestation of the Spirit. The word manifestation (*phanerosis*) indicates something being displayed or disclosed. It means to announce, reveal, or to show something off. What is being disclosed? Better stated, *who* is being disclosed? Who is being manifested through each of us? The answer is the Holy Spirit.

Greater Manifestations of the Spirit

You are to be an instrument that God uses to constantly display the work of the Holy Spirit. These manifestations are not about you, but they disclose the activity of the Spirit. They always point to Him. Finally, Paul said that the manifestation of the Spirit is for the common good. The word good (*symphero*) can be translated "profitable," but it means to stand side by side with someone to hold them up. So, when the Spirit's manifestations occur through you, they strengthen and build up people around you. A healthy church is one where the manifestations of the Spirit are occurring through the people on all occasions.

Paul identified nine manifestations in this passage (1 Corinthians 12:8-10). It's clear from 1 Corinthians 12:7 that a manifestation is *given* by the Holy Spirit. In Galatians 5:22-23, Paul identified the fruit of the Holy Spirit, and fruit is *grown*. Both, the fruits and the manifestations are the result of the Holy Spirit. Fruit and manifestations (functions) are not "worked up" in the flesh. If you are filled with the Holy Spirit, then eventually your life will grow fruit—nine fruits to be exact in Galatians. Likewise, if you are filled with the Holy Spirit, then you become an instrument that God can give manifestations to—nine functions in 1 Corinthians 12:8-10.

Let's talk about the potential of manifestations for a moment. Someone once said to me, "I just want His presence in my life. I'm not interested in His power." That's not possible because if you have the Holy Spirit in your life, then power will be released through you. Without power exuding from your life, we might question if you are actually filled with the Spirit. Jesus said, "You will receive power when the Holy Spirit has come upon you; . . ." (Acts 1:8a).

One of the best definitions for power (*dynamis*) that I've read is a manifesting influence over all reality in a supernatural manner. The Holy Spirit will always be demonstrated through you if you are filled with the Spirit and compliant to His leadership. It *is* possible to mistreat the Holy Spirit. You can blaspheme the Spirit (Matthew 12:31), resist the Spirit (Acts 7:51), grieve the Spirit (Ephesians 4:30), and quench the Spirit (1 Thessalonians 5:19).

It's not advisable, however, to mistreat the Holy Spirit. Instead, it's better to cooperate with the Spirit and release His power wherever we might be. You might be in a factory, hospital, coffee shop, grocery store, or sitting in a church gathering. It makes no difference where you might be. If you are filled with the Holy Spirit, then you become an instrument for His power and manifestations to work through.

Additionally, power and manifestations can increase because we can have increases of the Holy Spirit. I believe that each day there can be an increase in the carrying capacity of the Spirit and His power in our lives. Some people have argued with me, stating that He gets more of us rather than us getting more of Him. I'm not interested in debating the subject, but when I investigate the Bible, it seems to state that greater outpourings of the Holy Spirit were given.

For example, in Acts 13:52 it says, "And the disciples were continually filled with joy and with the Holy Spirit." The phrase "continually filled" is an imperfect verb that represents continuous or reoccurring action in the past. They were not merely filled once, but it continued to occur over and over again. It would be safe to ask whether you are increasing in the Holy Spirit each day or not. Jesus stated that we could have much more of the Spirit if we asked (Luke 11:13), and John stated that the Spirit is given without measure (John 3:34). How much do you want?

I believe that each day we can receive a fresh touch of the Holy Spirit in our lives. So, if the Spirit is increasing, then so are power and manifestations. And if power and manifestations are increasing, then the ability to strengthen and build up people around you increases, too. Who wouldn't desire that?

People in our cities, communities, and churches desperately need to be built up. They need someone filled with the Spirit manifesting His power that alters their reality in a supernatural manner. Open up your life and heart to a fresh baptism of the Holy Spirit. Allow your life to become an instrument in His hands (Romans 6:13) that He can continually fill with the Spirit, and then let Him manifest His Spirit through you to profit everyone around you.

PRAYER

Father, I pray for a fresh increase of your Holy Spirit today. I cry out for a fresh baptism of your Spirit so that I can become the instrument you use to manifest your presence. I want to build people up and minister to them through the power of your Spirit, in Jesus' name, amen.

APPLICATION

1. Have you witnessed any of the nine manifestations identified in 1 Corinthians 12:8-10 operating through you? If so, describe.
2. How much are you willing to press in for more of the Holy Spirit in your life?
3. How has the Holy Spirit used you to minister to someone around you? Describe.
4. Begin to ask for joy and the Holy Spirit every day.

39

A Spirit of Revelation

Revelation means to remove the veil and to expose the truth.

A prayer that has captured my heart and is prayed almost daily comes from the words of Paul in Ephesians. He asked, "That the God of our Lord Jesus Christ, the Father of glory, may give to you a spirit of wisdom and of revelation in the knowledge of Him" (Ephesians 1:17). That is a profound request that I hope will consume your prayers.

The word revelation (*apokalupsis*) is a compound word. The root word (*kalupsis*) means to conceal or to hide and the prefix means to remove, uncover, or take off. Satan desires to keep God's people in spiritual darkness. He blinds their eyes and keeps the truth of the gospel hidden from their eyes (2 Corinthians 4:4). Revelation, then, means to remove the veil and to expose the truth. Without divine illumination we would remain blind and ignorant to spiritual things, and the word of the cross would sound foolish to us (1 Corinthians 1:18).

Revelation is what enabled the apostle Paul to preach the gospel with boldness. He received the gospel *not* from a human being but through revelation (Galatians 1:12). That's why he didn't need to consult with flesh and blood about his calling. Paul had his eyes opened to spiritual truths through an encounter with the Holy Spirit, and as a result he was impervious to what people thought (Galatians 1:16).

Through revelation spiritual mysteries were made known to Paul (Ephesians 3:3), and he wrote to the Corinthians, stating that their eyes, ears, and hearts hadn't grasped what God had in store for them. But through revelation the Spirit was going to make those blessings known to them (1 Corinthians 2:9–10).

Revelation is one of the functions of the Spirit according to Jesus. He said, "But when He, the Spirit of truth, comes, He will guide you into all truth; . . . " (John 16:13a). Imagine that! The Holy Spirit, through His guidance and revelation, will lead us into *all* truth. Jesus went on to say that the Spirit will take everything that belongs to the Father and "disclose" it to us (John 16:14–15).

Little wonder then that Jesus said, "To you it has been granted to know the mysteries of the kingdom of heaven" (Matthew 13:11). Jesus concluded by stating that we would see and hear things that many prophets of old never had the privilege of receiving because they were not able to be filled with the Spirit like we are. This is one of the blessings of a spirit of revelation in the new covenant.

I believe that revelation is ongoing throughout our lifetime if we'll remain in the Spirit. I've had people tell me that

A Spirit of Revelation

truth is truth, and once we know God's truth, there is no expansion of that truth. I don't believe that, and it doesn't make sense either. Our understanding of truth can always increase. Truth is layered like lasagna, and the Spirit knows when we're ready to carry greater revelation.

Jesus implied an increase of revelation when He said to His disciples, "I have many more things to say to you, but you cannot bear them now" (John 16:12). In other words, they didn't have the spiritual fortitude and stamina to carry a greater revelation at that moment, but once they were cleansed and filled with the Spirit, greater revelations would come.

Let me suggest a few obvious things that will increase revelation in our lives. First, stay in the Spirit (Galatians 5:25). Revelation is a blessing of a Spirit-filled life, so remain in the Spirit if you desire greater revelation.

Second, immerse yourself in the Word of God. The Scriptures were inspired, literally "breathed to life," by the Spirit (2 Timothy 3:16). By constantly immersing ourselves in the Bible, we will become saturated with a spirit of revelation.

Third, pray prayers that are led and influenced by the Spirit (Ephesians 6:18). Prayer is communion with God, and it's the essence of worship. To truly worship God, we must forget about ourselves, and to pray effectively we must focus completely on Him. Prayer and worship keep us exposed to the Spirit, and that keeps our minds attuned to revelation. Paul wrote, "But whenever a person turns to the Lord, the veil is taken away" (2 Corinthians 3:16). When we turn to the Lord, literally when we worship or focus on Him, He removes the cover from our eyes. Revelation always occurs in His presence.

Fourth and finally, Paul wrote, "Set your mind on the things above, not on the things that are on earth" (Colossians 3:2). Learn to live with a kingdom conscience and not a worldly conscience. Learn to seek first His kingdom in everything you do, and refuse to live with fear and anxiety, believing that God will provide for you (Matthew 6:33).

When Jesus came into the world, He came as a light of revelation (Luke 2:32). Among other things, He desired to open our eyes and to expose them to the light of the gospel. God desires that we not merely see clearer but that we hear, speak, think, and live differently. We are kingdom citizens sent as ambassadors of Christ to reconcile a world to God (Philippians 3:20 and 2 Corinthians 5:20).

But we will not fulfill our assignments without a spirit of revelation. We will not live with a heavenly perspective if revelation is not increasing in our lives. Additionally, I believe that there are songs to be written, messages to be preached, pictures to be painted, music to be orchestrated, poems to be penned, books to be printed, art to be sculpted, dances to be choreographed, and God-given dreams waiting to come to fruition, but all of these things are the result of the inspiration and revelation of the Holy Spirit. My encouragement to you is to do what is necessary to increase a spirit of revelation in your life.

PRAYER

Father, I pray that you would give me a spirit of wisdom and revelation. Open my eyes to deeper spiritual truths and expose my mind to kingdom realities. Thank you for increased insight in Jesus' name, amen.

APPLICATION

1. What is the Lord opening your eyes to? How can you share this revelation with others?
2. What are some new insights that the Holy Spirit has given you from the Bible?
3. What are some creative ways the Holy Spirit has spoken to you?
4. How can you receive even greater revelation from God?

40

Dying to Live

Dying to ourselves means to give our lives up to Christ. It means that He can do with our lives whatever He chooses because our lives belong to Him as a living sacrifice.

Did you know that the way to live in the kingdom is to die?

Obviously, I don't mean suicide or a natural death. I'm referring to spiritually dying to ourselves. Life in the kingdom of God is different from our natural perspective. It's been called the "kingdom paradox." The way to win is to lose, the way to be first is to be last, the way up is down, the way to lead is to serve, and the way to live is to die. The only way that Jesus can truly be visible is when we get out of His way.

The apostle Paul obviously understood that concept because he said in Galatians 2:20, "I have been crucified with Christ; and it is no longer I who live, but Christ lives in me; and the *life* which I now live in the flesh I live by faith in the

Son of God, who loved me and gave Himself up for me." Paul was referring to dying to his selfish flesh.

Moreover, he lived "dead to self" because he said, "the life which I now live in the flesh I live by faith in the Son of God." Paul's life was consumed by Christ, and his entire focus was on Christ, not on himself. He also wrote, "For to me, to live is Christ and to die is gain" (Philippians 1:21). In order for Paul to spiritually live, he had to die to his own selfish flesh. When it came time to die naturally, his life would gain an eternal inheritance with Christ.

"Then Jesus said to his disciples, 'If anyone wishes to come after Me, he must deny himself, and take up his cross and follow Me'" (Matthew 16:24). To deny ourselves is to disregard our own interests in comparison with Christ. His ways and His will are to always take precedence over our lives. Denying ourselves is humbling, and oftentimes it is very costly. Humbling ourselves goes against the grain of our culture, which actually is bent on self-pleasure. In order to deny ourselves, we will have to be willing to die to ourselves.

But what does it mean to die to ourselves? Dying to ourselves means to give our lives up to Christ. It means that He can do with our lives whatever He chooses because our lives belong to Him as a living sacrifice (Romans 12:1). However, dying to ourselves does *not* mean to disrespect our lives. It doesn't mean that we don't love ourselves. On the contrary, if we truly love our lives, we will place them into God's hands because only He can deliver us from the sin that corrupts and destroys our lives. If we truly value our lives, we will put them into the hands of the Creator and let Him do with them whatever He desires. This actually is the essence of living a sanctified life.

Walking in a life of sanctification and holiness goes beyond merely dying to ourselves one time. Part of maturing in sanctification is dying to ourselves whenever we sense our flesh wanting to resurrect. Going back to Jesus' words in Matthew 16:24, if we're going to follow Him, we will have to deny ourselves. Denying ourselves is part of dying to ourselves, and sometimes—many times—we find the need to do that daily.

Therefore, we have to "die to live" because when we are out of the way, Jesus can be seen. I want to get even more practical. Several years ago, I read seven statements that reflected the essence of dying to live. Read these statements aloud, prayerfully, and allow the Holy Spirit to challenge your heart. I read these often, and every time I do I'm challenged to die a deeper death so that I can personify Jesus even more.

1. When you are forgotten, neglected, or purposely avoided, and you don't sting or hurt with the insult or the oversight, but your heart is happy, being counted worthy to suffer for Christ—that is dying to live.
2. When your good is evil spoken of, when your wishes are crossed, your advice disregarded, your opinions ridiculed, and you refuse to let anger rise up your heart, or even defend yourself, but take it all in patient, loving silence—that is dying to live.
3. When you lovingly and patiently bear any disorder, any irregularity, any unpunctuality, or any annoyance; when you stand face to face with waste, folly,

extravagance, and spiritual insensibility, and endure it as Jesus endured—that is dying to live.

4. When you are content in all circumstances—any food, any offering, any climate, any society, any apparel, or any interruption by the will of God, and you never sulk, whine, complain, become moody, or entice the attention of others—that is dying to live.
5. When you never care to refer to yourself in conversation, to record your own good works, or to itch after commendations; when you can truly love to be unknown—that is dying to live.
6. When you can see your brother prosper and observe his needs being met and can honestly rejoice with him in spirit and feel no envy, nor question God while your own needs are far greater and in more desperate circumstances—that is dying to live.
7. When you can receive correction and reproof from one of less standing than yourself, and can humbly submit inwardly as well as outwardly, finding no rebellion or resentment rising up within your heart—that is dying to live.[7]

Which of these statements speak to you? Allow the Holy Spirit to move deeper through your heart and life. May we all truly die to live, and may we echo the apostle Paul's words, "I have been crucified with Christ; . . . Christ lives in me." (Galatians 2:20).

PRAYER

Take my life, God. Consume me until the only thing people see is you. Live through me and possess my very being and touch this world through my life. I pray in Jesus' name, amen.

APPLICATION

1. What do you think it means to die to yourself?
2. Re-read the seven statements. Is there something in your life that you need to die to?
3. At what cost are you willing to die to your flesh so that the Holy Spirit can flow through you? Have you given your entire life to God with no conditions? If not, what holds you back?
4. Do you believe that you are dying a deeper death to selfish flesh each day? Why or why not?

41

Houses of Prayer

If we're going to become houses of prayer, Jesus might need to overturn some of the activities of our churches.

Many years ago, I bought and read every book written by Leonard Ravenhill. I'm not certain that Ravenhill would be welcome in many of our churches today. His passionate call to prayer wouldn't rest well with those who don't burn for revival. In *Revival God's Way*, Ravenhill likened the church to a sleeping sentry because after being charged with the task of guarding our citadels, we fell asleep on the wall. Therefore, the enemy has gained access into our churches.

I had the privilege of hearing him speak, and his message was as convicting as his books. He described a vision that he had of large billows of smoke rising from the earth into the heavens but contrasted that with a small wisp of smoke rising to the heavens. The Holy Spirit spoke to Ravenhill and said, "The large billows of smoke represent the amount of sin, immorality, and iniquity that is rising up from the earth.

The small wisp of smoke is the amount of intercession being lifted to the heavens by the Church."[8] It's little wonder then that the enemy has crept into our cities, churches, families, and homes. I'm reminded of Paul's words, "Awake, sleeper, and arise from the dead" (Ephesians 5:14).

One much greater than Ravenhill, however, confronted the powerless church in Matthew chapter 21. Passover week brought two and a half million people together in Jerusalem, and the city surged with religious expectations. It was in the midst of this incredible, significant Jewish celebration that Jesus entered the city. As the crowds screamed, "Hosanna to the Son of David," the entire city buzzed with excitement. Nonetheless, Jesus was not impressed with the shallow worship. Regardless of the glorious celebration, there was trouble in the temple.

What I find interesting about this passage is that Jesus entered the city with a mission. He knew where the central problem was, and He was there to make things right. It is no different today. The problem in our cities rests upon the church. I once heard Rhonda Hughey say that if our cities are filled with immorality, corruption, sin, and strongholds, then it indicates that the church has abdicated its position of authority to the enemy. Jesus always looks to the church because we are the hope of the world. If the church is not what she should be, our cities will never be transformed. Likewise, our worship will sound just as hollow as it did that day in Jerusalem.

The Bible says, "And Jesus entered the temple and drove out all those who were buying and selling in the temple, and overturned the tables of the money changers and the seats of those who were selling doves" (Matthew 21:12). Please keep in mind that those people were offering religious services. In other words, they were supposed to be there. They were providing services to those needing to purchase a sacrifice for use in the temple and to exchange secular currency for temple currency.

Therefore, those selling doves and the money changers were part of the religious milieu of the hour. Yet, those activities prevented the essential ministry of God's house from taking place. Let me be clear: if we're going to become houses of prayer, Jesus might need to overturn some of the activities of our churches. This doesn't mean that what we are doing is wrong, but sometimes we are so busy doing *our* business that we don't have time to do *God's* business—to pray.

Jesus then declared, "My house shall be called a house of prayer; but you are making it a robbers' den" (Matthew 21:13). It's not a house of sermons, a house of music, a house of programs, or a house of Bible studies. All of those activities have their place, but I would argue that they exude from one central activity. Jesus defined His house by the activity of prayer (*proseuche*). This word in its various forms is used one 127 times in the New Testament.

The prefix of *proseuche* is *pros*, and it tells us that this kind of prayer is "face to face." This word for prayer implies intimacy with God. Jesus was calling His church to become a house of lovers. He wanted a people so captivated by God's love that they would hunger to interact with Him day and night. When this becomes the central activity of the church, we'll be enabled to touch a city for God. If the church neglects its face-to-face interaction with God, then the atmosphere of our churches will become like a "den of thieves," offering no hope to anyone.

Note the next verse, "And *the* blind and *the* lame came to Him in the temple, and He healed them" (Matthew 21:14). The conjunction "and" can be translated "then," telling us that when Jesus becomes the central love of our hearts and we cry out to Him day and night (Luke 18:7), extraordinary activities will start to take place. A house of prayer always leads to spiritual transformation, and people will eventually be drawn to His manifest presence.

My challenge to all of us is to allow Jesus to overturn the activities in our churches that prevent us from becoming houses of prayer. Let Him have His way in cleaning out or removing what hinders intimate prayer. Allow Him to remove the "Martha ministries" so that we can sit at His feet like Mary and listen to His Word (Luke 10:39–40).

This challenge, though, extends beyond the local church. Every person reading this is to be a "house of prayer." Paul said, "Your body is a temple [a house of God] of the Holy Spirit who is in you, . . ." (1 Corinthians 6:19a). You are the walking house of prayer that is to pray without ceasing (1 Thessalonians 5:17). Perhaps Jesus will need to overturn some things in your life so that you can get face to face with God. Jesus will not be content until He gets to the "heart" of the issue in our lives.

We need to let Him clean our houses. We need to let Him sweep through our hearts and toss out the good to make room for God. When that happens, I believe that every one of us can become the instrument that He will use to touch, heal, and restore people inside and outside of the church walls. I'm encouraged by the resurgence of prayer across our land. Let's hold our position. Let's remain on our post. Let's not be found doing activities that haven't been assigned to us by Jesus. Let's not be found sleeping on the wall.

PRAYER

Father God, your desire is to have houses of prayer. Awaken your bride and prompt her to begin crying out again for your manifest presence. Teach me how to pray without ceasing, in Jesus' name, amen.

APPLICATION

1. Define the characteristics of what a house of prayer would like in your local church.
2. What changes will your church need to make to become a house of prayer? Are you willing to pay the price?
3. Is your own heart a house of prayer? Why or why not?
4. What activities in your life need to be overturned so that your life will be based on the foundation of prayer?

42

The Faith to Pray

Prayer is central to everything that we do, and all ministries must flow out of our intercession.

One day Jesus' disciples requested something of Him that I believe is very essential. They said, "Increase our faith" (Luke 17:5). That's an excellent request, isn't it? Don't we all have room for more faith in our lives? On the heels of their request, Jesus likened their faith to a mustard seed (Luke 17:6).

In Matthew's gospel, Jesus used the idea of a mustard seed again. "He presented another parable to them, saying, 'The kingdom of heaven is like a mustard seed, which a man took and sowed in his field; and this is smaller than all *other* seeds, but when it is full grown, it is larger than the garden plants and becomes a tree, so that the BIRDS OF THE AIR come and NEST IN ITS BRANCHES'" (Matthew 13:31–32).

Faith, much like the kingdom, must be sown to produce something extraordinary. So, without works, faith is dead (James 2:17). Yet, when we sow what God has given us—putting our faith to work—there will always be an increase. In fact, Jesus indicated that the kingdom of heaven initially appears small and insignificant, but when sown, the kingdom will be large enough that others will find rest (the birds of the air will nest in the branches). Faith, therefore, must grow like a mustard seed until its influence touches the lives of many people.

Let's look at another passage that might seem like we're changing gears but keep reading. The Bible says, "Now He was telling them a parable to show that at all times they ought to pray and not to lose heart" (Luke 18:1). The purpose of this parable was to inspire prayer, and the contrast is simple: pray or lose heart (*enkakeo*), which literally means to become so depleted of hope you are immobilized by discouragement.

We are to pray at all times, Jesus said. Every occasion is an opportunity for prayer. Prayer is central to everything we do, and all ministries must flow out of our intercession. Even Jesus modeled this by pushing the crowds away from time to time to enter the chamber room with the Father (Matthew 14:23; Luke 5:15-16). If we don't persevere in prayer, not only will ministries fail, but we'll lose heart and give up because of no hope. I can't begin to count the people who have left the ministry due to discouragement, but I can tell you that those whom I'm aware of didn't devote themselves to a lifestyle of prayer.

The parable that Jesus told in Luke 18:2-5 was quite simple. An unrighteous judge who neither feared God nor respected people was bombarded by a widow seeking legal protection. After her perseverance the judge finally said to himself, "Yet because this widow bothers me, I will give her legal protection, otherwise by continually coming she will wear me out" (Luke 18:5). "And the Lord said, 'Hear what the unrighteous judge said; now, will not God bring about justice for His elect who cry to Him day and night, and will He delay long over them? I tell you that He will bring about justice for them quickly. . . .'" (Luke 18:6–8a).

Obviously, if an unrighteous judge responded to a widow, though he didn't value human life, then how much more will a loving Father respond to His elect (*eklektos*, those personally chosen or hand-picked)? There is no comparison: our Father will quickly move on our behalf.

According to Jesus, the Father's response toward us is attached to this phrase: "who cry to Him day and night" (Luke 18:7). The word cry (*boao*) is a present tense verb indicating that it doesn't stop. It means to cry out, to shout aloud, or to utter a desperate scream. That doesn't sound very appealing to people these days. That's probably why there aren't enough prayer meetings surrounded by the desperate cries of God's people. Perhaps we've become too dignified and satisfied to cry out.

I realize that "crying out" isn't the only style of prayer, but it's the one that Jesus identified in this passage. I've had people tell me, "I'm just not comfortable crying out." My general response is that they aren't *desperate* enough for His presence or for His transformation to cry out. I usually explain that if their house was ablaze and their children were concealed in a bedroom about to be consumed by the fire, they wouldn't calmly request help from someone. How much more do we need God's Holy Spirit to move on our churches, our cities, or our country? How desirous are we to see corporate revival?

It was the cries of a desperate Syrophoenician woman that captured Jesus' attention (Matthew 15:22). It was the cries of two blind men outside Jericho that made Jesus stop (Matthew 20:31). It was the cries of blind Bartimaeus that ushered his own healing (Mark 10:47-48). Isaiah wrote, "Then you will call, and the Lord will answer; you will cry, and He will say, 'Here I am'" (Isaiah 58:9). God always shows up to the cries of His people because our cries usually demonstrate our posture of humility and brokenness, and it's in that position we're most ready to be touched and used by God.

By using the phrase "day and night," Jesus indicated our willingness to persevere. We all desire immediate results because that's the culture in which we live, and sometimes we've had the blessing of instantaneous answers to our prayers. But I believe Jesus was underscoring the necessity of ongoing, consistent prayers until the breakthrough is experienced. Too many prayer meetings have fizzled because of a lack or perseverance, and too many unanswered prayers have been accepted by discouraged followers who failed to cry out day and night until they saw results. Don't quit! Don't stop! Stay on the wall and cry out day and night: never keep silent (Isaiah 62:6).

It's interesting to note how Jesus ended His lesson, "However, when the Son of Man comes, will He find faith on the earth" (Luke 18:8b)? Wait a minute, is Jesus talking about

The Faith to Pray

prayer or faith? Yes! Which is it? The answer is both. It takes faith to persevere day and night until we see the response that we're petitioning God for. Persevering prayer is an indicator of faith because it means that we're tenaciously looking into the heavenly realm to apprehend something that we are confident will manifest in the earthly realm. "Now faith is the assurance of things hoped for, the conviction of things not seen" (Hebrews 11:1).

The prayer Jesus talked about in Luke 18 carries the same idea: we persevere in prayer because we have the assurance of things we're praying for, and this produces a conviction in our hearts to cry out day and night until it breaks forth. Faith, like prayer, is a seed that must be sown, and if we'll sow into the Spirit and not lose heart, we will reap a great harvest (Galatians 6:8–9). When Jesus asked if He'll find faith on earth, maybe He's asking if He'll find people praying! Either way, I want my faith and prayers to increase like a seed planted in a garden because I'm confident that the end result will be huge.

PRAYER

Lord, burn in me a desire to have faith to pray for the impossible, even if I can't see it. Give me the perseverance to pray without ceasing for things that are important to you.

APPLICATION

1. How desperate are your prayers?
2. Are you willing to cry out in prayer day and night for a breakthrough in your life? What about for the breakthrough in someone else's life?
3. Do you believe that your faith and prayers are increasing? Why or why not?
4. When the Son of Man returns, will He find your church contending in prayer?

43

The Breath of Intercession

Perhaps the early church merely started "breathing" on the day of Pentecost, which enabled them to function with power.

Is God truly the air that we breathe?

There's an interesting verse that I've been trying to wrap my head around in Numbers. God was defending Moses to Miriam and Aaron. He described Moses as a prophet like no other, and then God stated: "With him I speak mouth to mouth" (Numbers 12:8a). God didn't speak to Moses in visions, riddles, and mysteries like the other prophets; rather, His dialogue with Moses was so intimate that they were mouth to mouth with each other.

I envision someone being resuscitated by CPR, which is a mouth-to-mouth procedure. Quite possibly the only way someone who stopped breathing might survive is if they are given mouth-to-mouth resuscitation. Maybe that is a picture of how we are to live moment by moment with God. Maybe

He is the air that we breathe, and our very survival is by mouth-to-mouth intercession with God. If Moses breathed mouth to mouth with God in an inferior covenant, just imagine what is possible when we are filled with the breath of the Holy Spirit in the new covenant.

When we speak about the Holy Spirit, in essence, we are speaking about the sacred breath of God. Spirit (*pneuma*) is translated breath or air. I realize that the Holy Spirit is a person, and I take nothing from that. Yet, He came as a mighty rushing wind at Pentecost, and they were all filled with the Spirit (Acts 2:1-4). Perhaps the early church merely started "breathing" on the day of Pentecost, which enabled them to function with power.

Think about every breath you take: are you breathing *only* air or is it the breath of God? We are told that God breathed into the nostrils of mankind, and he became a living being at that moment (Genesis 2:7). Jews believe that with every breath we take, we are stating the Hebrew name of God (YHVH). Perhaps a person dies not when their heart stops but when they are no longer capable of saying His name, the name of God. Jesus actually breathed on His disciples, and they received the Spirit (John 20:22). Perhaps Jesus released the breath of God upon them.

In 1 Thessalonians 5:17, Paul stated: "Pray without ceasing." I love to study the New Testament language. Yes, I'm a word nerd. I have studied this verse over and over again. Guess what it means? It means to "pray without ceasing." It's true: we are to *always* be in a state of intercession. I believe

The Breath of Intercession

that if we understand living mouth to mouth with God, we can capture the heart of intercession.

Prayer really should never end for the person who walks in the Spirit. We are to devote our lives to prayer (Colossians 4:2), and praying without ceasing is only possible if we remain in the Spirit, breathing mouth to mouth with God. Therefore, every breath we take can become a moment that we consume the presence of the Spirit—thus enabling communion with God every second of our day. Regardless of what occurs to us, we can remain in constant connection to God as we breathe Him in.

Paul and Silas were thrown into prison while ministering in the city of Philippi. After having cast out a spirit of divination from woman, the profit from her satanic activity diminished and so her owners were angry. Paul and Silas were stripped and beaten with rods, and after many blows, they were thrown into the "inner" prison with their feet fastened to stocks (Acts 16:14-30). The inner cell was a hole in the floor below the prison, and scholars believe it was nothing more than a sewage pit filled with excrement from the city.

The word used in Acts 16:24 referring to the inner (*esoteros*) prison actually means the space behind the veil. It can be translated the Holy of Holies. Some commentators call this the place of encounter. The same word "inner" is used only one other time in the New Testament. Hebrews 6:19-20a says, "This hope we have as an anchor of the soul, a *hope* both sure and steadfast and one which enters within the veil, where Jesus has entered as a forerunner for us, ..." When the writer says that we enter "within," it refers to the Holy of

Holies; the place of encounter with Christ. This is the same word used in Acts 16:24 referring to the dark and filthy cesspool where Paul and Silas found themselves.

However, for the person who is breathing in the Holy Spirit—the one who is mouth to mouth with God every moment of his or her life—what might be a prison on the outside is actually a place of supernatural encounter with Jesus Christ. The earthly circumstances that we find ourselves in become the place where divine activity takes place because when we breathe in His Spirit every moment, we're never out of His presence, power, or potential.

Guess what Paul did while being strapped ankle deep in sewage? He prayed and sang praises unto God. Think about it, for Paul and Silas they were in the Holy of Holies! And other prisoners heard the worship, which tells me that other people are watching and listening to our response when persecution and adversity come upon us.

Suddenly, the prison house was shaken, and every prisoner found themselves unshackled (Acts 4:31). When we live mouth to mouth with God, our lives become the instruments He can use to set others free. The prisoners didn't flee the scene, however. They remained in the worship service, and eventually the jailer cried out: "What must I do to be saved?" Salvation came to a stench-filled hole in the ground because two guys lived mouth to mouth with God. Paul and Silas were praying without ceasing, and their intercession turned a prison into a sanctuary.

Let Him become the air you breathe and watch what will happen.

PRAYER

Lord, my desire is to be so close to you that I live mouth to mouth with you. Let every breath from my mouth be pleasing to you. Help me to worship in and through all the circumstances that I may find myself in, amen.

APPLICATION

1. Describe what an intimate relationship looks like with God. How can you practically live mouth to mouth with Him?
2. Take a moment to breathe and think about God breathing His breath into you. Can you feel the presence of God all around you?
3. What are some ways that you can stay in a posture of worship when chaos abounds?
4. How can you learn to pray without ceasing?

44

Destroying Strongholds

Spiritual warfare is really a battle for your mind; it's a battle of what you will come into agreement with.

Where is Satan's throne room?

I heard someone once say: "Satan's throne room is wherever a lie is believed." You may not like that answer, but I have to agree with it. The only real power that the enemy has over our lives is what we give him. When you believe a lie, you empower the liar.

Jesus said of the enemy, "[He] does not stand in the truth because there is no truth in him. Whenever he speaks a lie, he speaks from his own *nature*, for he is a liar and the father of lies" (John 8:44b). Spiritual warfare is really a battle for your mind; it's a battle of what you will come into agreement with. Will you agree with God's Word, which is truth (John 17:17), or will you align yourself to the enemy's delusions?

Whatever occupies your mind directs your life. Believing lies over a course of time will establish a spiritual stronghold in your mind. Ed Silvoso defined a stronghold this way: "A spiritual stronghold is a mindset impregnated with hopelessness that causes us to accept as unchangeable, situations that we know are contrary to the will of God."[9]

In other words, we've believed the lies of the enemy to the point that all hope is lost. We give up and give in to the idea that things will never change. We believe that we'll never be healed, we'll never get out of the mess, our children will never be saved, or we'll never be free from this addiction. Even though God can and will bring transformation in our lives, our minds have become impregnated with hopelessness. We've become bound by deception.

The word "stronghold" is used one time in the New Testament. It's found in 2 Corinthians 10:4 and is translated "fortresses" in the New American Standard Bible (NASB). A fortress (*ochuroma*) is a castle or a prison with high walls. Used in the context of this passage of Scripture, it describes a prison where someone is held captive and is surrounded by very high walls. Paul actually described in these verses how fortresses (strongholds) are built. He said, "*We are* destroying speculations and every lofty thing raised up against the knowledge of God, . . ." (2 Corinthians 10:5a).

"Speculations" describe imaginations, reasoning, and thoughts, and "lofty things" refers to something elevated that shouldn't be. When the enemy speaks a lie, we should "take that thought captive" according to Paul (2 Corinthians 10:5). Once that thought has been brought before Christ, if it doesn't align to the Word, then we cast it out. The moment we entertain thoughts and imaginations that are contrary to God's Word, we start to build a wall. Over time, if we continue elevating lies above the knowledge of God, we will feel trapped, bound, and imprisoned in despair and hopelessness.

Too many people in churches aren't spiritually free. They are bound by lies and imprisoned by strongholds. Consequently, they live with fear and joylessness and seldom pray prayers of faith believing that God will bring the needed breakthrough. Jesus may have their hearts, but the enemy has influenced their minds. Can I tell you that you don't have to live that way? Jesus came with the anointing to set captives free (Luke 4:18).

Note these words from Paul, "For the weapons of our warfare are not of the flesh, but divinely powerful for the destruction of fortresses" (2 Corinthians 10:4). You have been equipped with the power of God to destroy, demolish, annihilate, and obliterate the wall of lies. You don't stand against the enemy in your flesh, but you stand against him in the mighty power of God. You've been equipped to, as Paul said, "Put on the full armor of God, so that you will be able to stand firm against the schemes of the devil" (Ephesians 6:11).

Paul said in Philippians 4:7, "And the peace of God . . . will guard your hearts and your minds in Christ Jesus." Think about that for a moment. His presence actually watches over our minds. God is like a sentinel who oversees everything that enters our minds. Therefore, when a thought or an impression doesn't line up to the Word, we're going to know it because the Spirit of God will alert us. It's at that moment that we are to take authority over that thought, impression, or suggestion that is incongruent with truth and throw it out of our minds. You have been given the power of the Holy Spirit to think correctly.

Additionally, fill your mind with the Word of God because if you know the truth, then you will more easily recognize a lie. Paul said, "Finally, brethren, whatever is true, whatever is honorable, whatever is right, whatever is pure, whatever is lovely, whatever is of good repute, if there is any excellence and if anything worthy of praise, dwell on these things" (Philippians 4:8). If you are dwelling on news and events of our day or if you are listening to gripes, complaints, and negativity, then you will be more susceptible to believing lies.

Your mind is like the control center of your spiritual life: you *are* what you think (Proverbs 23:7). Through the power of the Holy Spirit and the blood of Jesus, demolish and destroy all strongholds in your life. Learn to tear down the wall of lies and deception. Make your mind the throne room of God by walking in alignment to what His Word says about you and your life. Keep your eyes on Jesus (Hebrews 12:2) and your mind filled with Him, and you will walk in perfect peace (Isaiah 26:3).

PRAYER

Jesus, I repent for agreeing with lies. I repent for elevating other things above your Word. Cleanse and purify my mind and fill it with your truth. With your power help me to take every thought captive to the obedience of Christ, in Jesus' name, amen.

APPLICATION

1. What do you believe a stronghold is? Have you ever been bound by a stronghold?
2. What are some things that occupy your thoughts on a daily basis that are not in alignment with Christ's thoughts?
3. What are some things that you can do to keep your mind free from wrong thinking?
4. If you are bound by a stronghold, take authority over that now. Repent for agreeing with a lie and decree in Jesus' name that your mind will be freed from all lies. Learn to take every thought to Jesus for evaluation.

45

Breaking the Power of Offense

If you are crucified with Christ and you have died to yourself, then you really can't be trapped by an offense.

In Paul's second letter to Timothy, he wrote about those who were trapped by the enemy. He actually referred to "the snare of the devil" (2 Timothy 2:26). The word snare (*pagis*) refers to a trap, lasso, or noose. This word describes how birds are suddenly entangled and caught in a net. One of the greatest traps the enemy uses against God's people is an offense. "Then He said to his disciples, 'It is impossible that no offenses should come'" (Luke 17:1 NKJV). One of these days you're going to be challenged with an offense. Someone is going to say or do something that hurts you, and if you don't remain in the Spirit, you will be ensnared by the offense.

The word offense (*skandalon*) can be translated trap. It actually refers to the stick or trigger *in* the trap. This same word can be translated "stumbling block" because if one becomes trapped by an offense, they will usually stumble into spiritual problems or even into sin.

What is so disheartening to me is the amount of offense that occurs in churches. People leave churches over an offense. They quit ministry teams, they quit tithing, they quit worship groups, and they quit going to church because they've been offended. The services are too long, or they're too short. The messages aren't good, the music isn't right, the seats aren't comfortable, the people aren't friendly, and on it goes. I had someone leave my church because they were "offended" with the curtains. They thought the curtains were too drab for the sanctuary.

People can also become offended with Jesus. John the Baptist was in prison for his boldness against King Herod. During his imprisonment, he started wondering if Jesus was the Messiah or not. His circumstances actually overshadowed what he once knew for sure. When John the Baptist first saw Jesus, he declared Him to be the One who takes away sins (John 1:29), but the walls of his prison seemed greater than his knowledge of Jesus at the moment. So, he sent his disciples to Jesus and asked Him if He was the Expected One (Luke 7:20).

Jesus answered, "Go and report to John what you have seen and heard" (Luke 7:22). Jesus went on to describe healing, miracles, signs, and wonders, and He assured John that the gospel was being preached to the poor and great things were taking place. Jesus was confirming to John that He was the Messiah, but just before John's disciples left, Jesus added this: "Blessed is he who does not take offense at Me"

(Luke 7:23). In other words, "Tell John not to get trapped by his circumstances. I'm still the Messiah even though he's in prison and even if he remains in prison."

Our circumstances don't dictate who Jesus is. He's still the miracle worker even though we haven't been healed. He's still the Lord of the breakthrough even though our circumstances seem difficult. He *is* the Messiah no matter what our circumstances are. However, will we become offended with Him? Will we get trapped by an offense over what we think Jesus should or should not do?

I believe it's His will to heal, but I haven't seen everyone I pray for healed yet. I believe it's His will that everyone come to repentance, but I have some friends who are running *away* from God. Sometimes my circumstances feel like a dingy, dark prison, but I can't become offended with Christ.

People can become offended with the Word, too. Jesus preached a challenging Word in John chapter 6. When He finished His message, many of His disciples simply had enough. "Therefore many of His disciples, when they heard this said, 'This is a difficult statement; who can listen to it?' But Jesus, conscious that His disciples grumbled at this, said to them, "Does this cause you to stumble" (John 6:60-61)? The word "stumble" also means to offend. Jesus wanted to know if His Word offended them like it did the others in the crowd that day.

His Word is truth (John 17:17), and sometimes that Word provokes us. Sometimes His Word insults our minds to capture our hearts. His Word is like a two-edged sword (Hebrews 4:12). It cuts to heal us, and it removes all the unnecessary debris. His Word equips and prepares us for every good work (2 Timothy 3:17). However, all of the blessings of God's Word will be stalemated if we become trapped by what He says and turn away from Him.

Over the years I've watched many people leave a gathering where the Word had been taught, but rather than repenting, they became ensnared in offense over the truth. In anger they resisted the transformation that God desired to bring into their lives.

The issue is not *if* you'll be offended. Jesus clearly said that offenses would come. The issue is will you become trapped by the offense? It's a terrible way to live — bound in offenses — because when we're trapped, we're easy prey for the enemy. The only solution I'm aware of is to relinquish your life to Jesus. If you are crucified with Christ and you have died to yourself, then you really can't be trapped by an offense.

Think about it this way: dead people cannot become ensnared by an offense. Say whatever you like to a dead person, but you won't get a response. I remember standing before the casket of my aunt, and it occurred to me that her blouse didn't match her scarf. She wouldn't have taken offense if I had said anything because she was dead.

In all actuality if you are trapped by any kind of an offense, then it's probably evidence that you haven't been crucified with Christ. Paul said, "I have been crucified with Christ; and it is no longer I who live, but Christ lives in me" (Galatians 2:20). A crucified life in Christ will not harbor offenses when they come. Someone completely filled with

Jesus will recognize the enemy's snare and avoid becoming caught by the noose. It's time to let go. It's time to forgive. It's time to die to yourself and let Jesus stuff you with Himself.

I decree and declare over you that you will be free from all offenses in Jesus' name.

PRAYER

Lord, search me and reveal to me any offenses that I am holding on to. Help me to let go of any offense against people, against the Word, or against God. I choose to live in a no offense zone. Thank you for freedom in Jesus' name, amen.

APPLICATION

1. Give yourself an "offense check-up." Is there anything or anyone that you have an offense against? If so, why?
2. Is there a phone call you need to make or a letter or email you need to write asking for forgiveness from someone? Do it as soon as possible.
3. What are some ways that you can guard against becoming offended?
4. Read and reread the first part of Galatians 2:20, "I have been crucified with Christ; and it is no longer I who live, but Christ lives in me." Ask the Lord to crucify your flesh.

46

Forgiveness

We will never be wronged by someone the way we have wronged God, and yet, God has wiped our debt free.

Some of the strongest teaching by Jesus focused on the topic of forgiveness. Jesus was approached by one of His disciples in Matthew 18:21 with this question: "Lord, how often shall my brother sin against me and I forgive him? Up to seven times?" I'm certain that Peter, who asked this question, anticipated a response by Jesus, such as, "Peter, your generosity of grace is so amazing! You've gone overboard with forgiveness."

The problem is, however, that Peter had a limit in mind as to the extent of forgiveness. He was drawing a line in the sand and was establishing a quota as to how far forgiveness would go. If one is focused on the limitations of forgiveness, then they are keeping a record of wrongs committed, which is a clear violation of love (1 Corinthians 13:5).

Jesus' response indicated that there are to be no limits or conditions of forgiveness. "Jesus said to him, 'I do not say to you, up to seven times, but up to seventy times seven'" (Matthew 18:22). Please put your calculators away! The response given by Jesus was essentially stating that there is never to be a time when forgiveness is *not* extended. We are to forgive no matter what, no matter when, and no matter how many times. To be clear, Jesus told a story that represents forgiveness from a kingdom perspective. I have discovered that the kingdom principles and our world's principles are in vast contrast to each other. That was true when Jesus taught this story, and I believe it to be true today.

As the story goes, when the king settled his accounts, he discovered someone who owed him ten thousand talents. That is equivalent to just over twelve million dollars. The slave could not repay that amount, so the king pronounced judgment on him and his family. He fell before the master and pleaded with him, and the Bible says, "And the lord of that slave felt compassion and released him and forgave him the debt" (Matthew 18:27). Amazing! The Bible says, ". . . But where sin increased, grace abounded all the more" (Romans 5:20b).

Our death sentence was paid in full by Jesus Christ. "He made Him who knew no sin *to be* sin on our behalf, so that we might become the righteousness of God in Him" (2 Corinthians 5:21). God's mercy and grace are outrageous, to say the least. His compassion is so extensive that He not only removes our debt, but He cleanses our hearts from the power of sin, which enables us to walk worthy of our calling in Christ.

With that backdrop in mind, Jesus continued. This same individual who had experienced forgiveness found his fellow servant who owed him a hundred denarii. How much is a hundred denarii? It is approximately seventeen dollars. Unmoved by his own experience of forgiveness, he grabbed his fellow servant by the throat and demanded full payment. No mercy was given, no compassion was extended, and no forgiveness was released. Because this fellow servant was unable to repay this debt, he was thrown into prison. What was initially distributed by the king to one person was not extended and released to another.

This kingdom principle of forgiveness was not grasped, and I'm saddened to say that this is still a problem among servants of the Lord. In many churches where I hold meetings, I'll find people who can't get "past the past." Something happened long ago that was wrong—incest, rape, abuse, mistreatment, or divorce—and the persons were deeply hurt or injured. Please know that I am not trivializing the pain that many people have experienced, but carrying the pain, burden, and offense for many years can be very destructive to the person.

Associated with an unforgiving heart, you will find anger and a deep-seated resentment toward a particular person or persons. Parents, children, spouses, or innocent bystanders become the target of our unresolved conflicts. Sometimes people are offended with God, believing that He didn't answer a particular prayer or move in a certain way that was anticipated. Add to all this the fact that our culture is steeped with retaliatory messages and ideologies through music, movies, and media that keep us in a constant state of agitation.

Many people possess the same mindset of Simon Peter. His question to Jesus revealed that he had a forgiveness quota you didn't want to cross. But think about this: we will never be wronged by someone the way we have wronged God, and yet,

God has wiped our debt free. Shouldn't our response toward others reflect the response we've received from God?

When the king discovered the truth about the slave, he was "moved with anger" (Matthew 18:34). It's interesting to note that the slave was not identified as "wicked" until he refused to forgive another person in the same manner he was forgiven.

The story ended with the slave who refused to forgive being handed over to the torturers. Jesus concluded, "My heavenly Father will also do the same to you, if each of you does not forgive his brother from your heart" (Matthew 18:35). The fact is forgiveness must reach our heart. Simply put, lip service will not do. We must release the offense, the hurt, the pain, and the sin that was caused to us. Unforgiveness will destroy our soul, mind, and even our bodies. I've actually seen people healed physically when they extended forgiveness.

Is there someone or something that you can't get free from? You will never be able to move ahead if you're tied to the past. Remember that you have experienced extraordinary grace from your Father in heaven; therefore, you've been empowered to give that away to others. Open your heart to God's mercy and grace once again. Allow His Holy Spirit to wash over you and enable you to extend what you've experienced.

It's time to let go of the offense and forgive.

PRAYER

Lord Jesus, because you have forgiven me from every sin, I choose to forgive those who have sinned against me. This very moment, I release the debt from my heart and declare that all is forgiven. I am released from all offenses, in Jesus' name, amen.

APPLICATION

1. Is there someone that you need to forgive? Do you need to forgive yourself?
2. Are there any conditions that you have put on forgiving someone?
3. Do you keep a record of wrongs that people have done to you? If so, will you ask God to destroy those records?
4. Why do you believe forgiveness is difficult for some people?
5. How can you learn to extend forgiveness to others quickly?

47

Breaking an Orphan Mindset

Spiritual orphans live in blindness or with a veil over their eyes. Consequently, they remain bound by a mindset of spiritual deficiency.

In an earlier lesson, we used Ed Silvoso's definition of a spiritual stronghold. He defined a stronghold as "a mindset impregnated with hopelessness that causes us to accept as unchangeable situations that we know are contrary to the will of God."[10] Almost every week I meet believers in churches who live and think as spiritual orphans. It's a terrible stronghold that keeps Christians believing that they're never good enough, that they never quite measure up, or that they haven't truly been accepted by God.

Jesus told His followers, "I will not leave you as orphans; I will come to you" (John 14:18). One expositor defined the word orphan (*orphanos*) as abandonment, obscurity, and being left in the darkness. Spiritual orphans feel a sense of abandonment and rejection despite the fact that God has chosen them. Apparently Jesus realized the tendency His disciples had of developing that mindset in His absence, so He reassured them that He was coming soon to abide with them and to be in them (John 14:17). Regardless of the fact that Jesus has sent His Spirit to cleanse and fill our hearts, there are many people bound by an orphan mindset who fail to recognize their full inheritance in Christ.

A story that identifies this mindset is Luke 15:11-32. A father had two sons, and the younger son came to the father and asked for his share of the estate. The father granted it to him and within a few weeks, the younger son left the father's home for a distant country. Sometime later there was a severe famine that occurred, and this young boy was in trouble because he had spent his share of the estate on loose living. He was so poor that he took a job feeding pigs, but to add insult, because of his hunger he desired to eat the pods that he fed to the pigs.

As he stood in the midst of this miserable mess, he came to his senses. The veil was removed from his eyes, and he realized that he had been very foolish. Repentance filled his heart, and he went back home in humility, not demanding sonship but rather choosing a position of a servant. His father wouldn't hear of it. Instead, he placed his best robe on his son, a ring on his finger, and sandals on his feet.

The father, out of love for his son who had returned, elevated him from poverty to royalty in a matter of minutes, and a party was thrown in his honor. As people danced and celebrated, the older son came in from the field. He refused to enter the celebration. I want to propose that he had an orphan mindset. In reality, he was as lost as the younger son had been even though he never left the father's side. Many spiritual orphans are in the church and are even near the presence of God, yet they are unable to experience the joy of being a son/daughter.

Let's identify five characteristics of an orphan mindset from this passage in Luke. First, spiritual orphans are often angry when others receive honor. The older son was angry and refused to join the party because he didn't think his brother was worthy of such honor (Luke 15:28). Spiritual orphans are unable to rejoice in the breakthrough that others receive for reasons such as jealousy, bitterness, offense, or envy. In this story, the older brother was angry and didn't believe his brother deserved such esteem.

Second, spiritual orphans find little joy in their ministry. "But [the older brother] answered and said to his father, 'Look! For so many years I have been serving you . . .'" (Luke 15:29a). The word serving (*douleuo*) is a present tense verb meaning to "continue slaving" for someone. The older son did not serve out of love. His service to the father was more of a duty than a delight. There is no lasting joy in the hearts of spiritual orphans because they see their ministry as an obligation and not a blessing.

Third, a spiritual orphan's attachment to the Father is usually based on what they do. The older son said, ". . . and I have never neglected a command of yours" (Luke 15:29b). He was calling attention to *his* works, *his* activities, *his* goodness, and *his* service because his sense of connection with the father was based solely on good behavior. We can only imagine that he was trying to gain the approval of his father. Spiritual orphans fail to recognize their identities as children of God, so they live much of their lives trying to impress God.

Fourth, spiritual orphans detach themselves from those they are angry with. The older son said, "But when this son of yours came" (Luke 15:30a). In other words, "He's not my brother." Spiritual orphans not only detach and distance themselves from those they are angry with, but they often surmise the evil or sin that others are involved in. Note that the older son said his brother wasted the father's wealth "with prostitutes" (Luke 15:30). The Bible doesn't actually say that the younger brother did that but only that he squandered his estate on "loose living," which means riotous or extravagant living. Spiritual orphans are good at assuming what others are doing, and often they contrive untrue stories about those they are angry with.

The fifth and final characteristic of a spiritual orphan is their inability to recognize their inheritance. They simply fail to recognize how they've been blessed. The father said to his son, "all that is mine is yours" (Luke 15:31). Think about that for a moment, this son was whining about one young goat to celebrate with his friends when he owned the entire farm. Spiritual orphans live in blindness or with a veil over their eyes. Consequently, they remain bound by a mindset of spiritual deficiency. In reality, the older son was living in spiritual poverty even while remaining in the presence of royalty.

This is a terrible way to live and certainly not what Jesus gave His life for. I want to pray that the veil is taken off the minds of all spiritual orphans. Our Father has given us a spirit of adoption, and we are privileged to cry out "Abba, Father," which actually is an intimate term that can be translated "papa" (Romans 8:14–15).

Take authority over this mindset in Jesus' name and demolish this stronghold. Come into agreement with the fact that you have been chosen and adopted as a son/daughter (Ephesians 1:5). You don't have to live as a spiritual orphan any longer. It's time to experience intimacy with the Father as a blessed child of the King.

PRAYER

Father, I repent of agreeing with an orphan mindset. I take authority over that mentality in Jesus' name, and I sever its hold over my mind. Thank you that I am your child and that you have blessed me with an eternal inheritance, amen.

APPLICATION

1. Can you identify any other characteristics of a spiritual orphan?
2. Do you have any tendencies of an orphan mindset? Why or why not?
3. Do you see yourself as the Father's chosen? If not, why?
4. How do you treat your brothers or sisters in Christ who dishonor the Lord? Are you able to rejoice with those who are blessed—even when it seems they aren't worthy of that blessing?

48

Extraordinary Power

It's not possible for the church to accomplish her mission without the power of the Holy Spirit operating in our lives.

Peter and John were on their way to a prayer meeting when they encountered a crippled man by the temple gate. The lame man was asking for alms, and he expected to receive something from the two disciples of Jesus. What he received, however, was beyond what he could have asked or imagined. "But Peter said [to the crippled beggar], 'I do not possess silver and gold, but what I do have I give to you: In the name of Jesus Christ the Nazarene—walk'" (Acts 3:6). What an incredible response! Peter released what he was most full of—namely, the power of God.

There's a story by Dennis Kinlaw that I shared in a previous lesson, but it bears repeating at this point. Kinlaw spoke of someone holding a glass of water in his hands and having someone else shake his arm. Of course, water spilled on the floor when his arm was shaken. When the question was asked about why water spilled, the obvious answer was given: "I shook your arm."

The question was asked yet again with emphasis, "Why did *water* spill?" At this point, people began to understand that what spilled from the glass was not determined by the shaking but by the contents. In every situation that confronts, squeezes, bumps, agitates, or challenges us, something will get released from our lives. What gets released from your life?

Peter was full of the Holy Spirit and His power. But the same potential is true for you and me, too. Jesus said, "But you will receive power when the Holy Spirit has come upon you; . . ." (Acts 1:8a). It's not possible to be full of the Holy Spirit and not have His power functioning within you and released out of you. This is why Jesus told His followers to remain in the city until they were "clothed with power" before venturing into ministry (Luke 24:49). Jesus knew that any ministry endeavor would be superfluous without power. He realized that His church could not advance forward and push back the gates of hell without power.

The early church functioned with enormous power. Years ago, a secular historian by the name of Ramsay MacMullen wrote a book called, *Christianizing the Roman Empire A.D. 100–400*. He was fascinated, from a historical point of view, by how the Roman Empire with its quest for power and obsession for false gods could crumble in the presence of simple followers of Jesus Christ. This Yale University professor's conclusion was that these believers functioned in a power that was greater than Rome had ever experienced before.[11]

That is why the early church experienced many wonders and signs (Acts 2:43). It is why there were no needy persons among them (Acts 2:34). It is why people lined up the sick on cots for Peter's shadow to fall on them and release healing as he walked by (Acts 5:15). It is why the church never quit preaching the message of Christ, why persecution only perpetuated the gospel, and why a layperson like Philip caused an entire city to rejoice (Acts 5:42; 8:4 and 6). I could go on and on, but the point remains that the early church was a church of power.

When Paul preached, it was more than just a good sermon. In fact, he declared, "And my message and my preaching were not in persuasive words of wisdom, but in demonstration of the Spirit and of power" (1 Corinthians 2:4). When he spoke to the church in Thessalonians he said, "For our gospel did not come to you in word only, but also in power and in the Holy Spirit and with full conviction; . . ." (1 Thessalonians 1:5a).

That same power is inside every believer today who is filled with the Holy Spirit. What does this power mean for you and me? Simply, it is a power to witness, a power to share the gospel, a power to lay hands on the sick, and a power to declare healing over people. This extraordinary power enables us to cast out demons, cleanse the lepers, and even raise the dead — activities that are normal for Jesus' followers (Matthew 10:7-8). This extraordinary power enables every Christ follower to walk in righteousness and holiness. Also, this power enables holy people to operate with supernatural gifts.

It's not possible for the church to accomplish her mission without the power of the Holy Spirit operating in our lives. We will never see explosive moves of God that transform churches and cities without the extraordinary power of the Holy Spirit. My prayer is that we will never become a church that holds to a form of godliness but denies its power (2 Timothy 3:5).

Paul warned us that this kind of demise would take place in the last days. Even the church in Galatia started out in the Spirit but later tried to operate in the flesh (Galatians 3:3). Think about your life, your ministry, and your church. Can it be described by extraordinary power? I've been provoked by this very question in my own life and ministry.

Let me close with a few suggestions. First, chase Jesus and not power. The absence of power can be a sign that we've been absent from His presence. Second, cry out for a fresh baptism of the Holy Spirit every day. We can be filled and "filling" each day. Third, live in the Word of God and especially read the Gospels and the book of Acts.

Fourth, follow His prompting every moment of your day. Jesus was filled with the Spirit, but He was "led" by the Spirit, too (Luke 4:1). Remain in a posture of obedience by allowing yourself to be led by the Spirit. Fifth, steward what you've been given. Don't ask for more of the Spirit if you're not attempting to release what you have been given. Give Jesus away to other people wherever you might be.

If Jesus is in you, then you carry His kingdom and His power. So, the next time you see someone in need, among other things give them the power of the Spirit.

PRAYER

Flow through me, Jesus. Fill me, use me, and empower me for your cause. May I be a conduit for God's power to operate through, amen.

APPLICATION

1. Can your life be defined in terms of supernatural power? Why or why not?
2. Describe someone that you know who is operating in the Holy Spirit's power.
3. In what ways can you release the supernatural extraordinary power of the kingdom around you every day?
4. When was the last time God used you to touch another person (or bless them, or pray for them, or release healing, or purchase something for them, etc.)?

49

Stagnant or Fresh

In our attempts to preserve the flow of God's Spirit, we inadvertently create paradigms around the activity of the Spirit.

I read a story written by Judy Franklin who contributed several chapters to the book entitled, *Walking in the Supernatural*.[12] This story was a vision she had about people gathering around a fountain drinking, splashing, and having a great time. The fountain was so strong at times that it would gush over the edges of the bowl, covering the ground.

As people observed the flow of water, someone said, "Let's go build a cistern to hold the water." Their statement, though logical, was made out of fear that one day the source would soon run dry, so the people dug a cistern and carried buckets of water until the cistern was full. When the cistern was filled, the people went about their lives and took their water from the cistern instead of the fountain.

However, the cistern had a very slow leak, and the people didn't realize that the water level was dropping. As time marched on, new people gathered around the cistern never realizing how full the cistern was previously. They assumed that it had always been at this present level. Over a long period of time, the water was reduced to mere puddles in the bottom of the cistern. People had to lie on the ground and reach into the cistern to get water, which had grown stagnant.

The people hadn't noticed that the water tasted foul because they had become dull to the taste of fresh, flowing water. Upon this realization, someone remembered the fountain, and everyone got excited and journeyed back to the original source. Of course, the water at the fountain was still flowing. People gathered around the fountain drinking, splashing, and having a great time. They were *revived* in the fresh flow of water. However, over time someone suggested that a cistern be built to preserve the water, and the cycle started all over again.

As I read this vision from Franklin, I couldn't help to think about how it reflects the move of the Spirit and revival in our churches. It reminds me of how revivals ebb because we drift from the main source. In our attempts to preserve the flow of God's Spirit, we inadvertently create paradigms around the activity of the Spirit. I made the statement one time that the greatest hindrance to the move of God was the move of God the week before. We cannot create a wineskin around the move of God's Spirit (Luke 5:37-39). Otherwise, it's like digging a cistern and relying on what God *did* and not on what He is *doing*.

Methods and strategies that we employ during an event or gathering that ushered the presence of God into a service

Stagnant or Fresh

must be loosely held in the next meeting. Otherwise, like the Pharisees, our traditions will become more sacred to us than the authentic activity of God's Spirit (Mark 7:13). How many needless battles have taken place in churches over human-constructed ideas that are thought to preserve the presence of God? Think about it: divisions have occurred over our "cisterns." Perhaps we're only serving stagnant water because we've long forgot what it's like to draw from the real source of life.

Jeremiah wrote, "For My people have committed two evils: They have forsaken Me, the fountain of living waters, To hew for themselves cisterns, Broken cisterns That can hold no water" (Jeremiah 2:13). Think about the progression of these two evils. First, we forsake God, the fountain of living waters. Through busyness, neglect, distraction, or even sinful activity, our intimate connection with God is impaired. I hear this same lament over and over again: "My life is so busy right now."

What takes precedence over your remaining connected to the source of life? Our lack of intimacy breeds spiritual assumptions, and it's not long before we commit the second evil of constructing ministries, plans, and ideas that when executed, don't carry the life-giving presence of the Holy Spirit. Anything we design, build, or hew that isn't inspired by the direct impulse of God will fail. Our churches will become broken-down cisterns that offer nothing but stagnant water.

Jesus said, "He who believes in Me, as the Scripture said, 'From his innermost being will flow rivers of living water'"

(John 7:38). Some scholars translate the "innermost being" as a womb, meaning that something is to spring to life from our spiritual womb—namely, rivers of *living* water. The water that springs forth from our lives is not to be stagnant but something that is full of vitality and life.

Additionally, this life-giving river is to "flow" from our inner being. This word carries the idea of water being constantly poured out or always flowing forth. The point that Jesus was making is that our lives should always flow with the life-giving presence of the Holy Spirit (John 7:39). Every person reading this should be a wellspring of life and hope to others. Our lives should be an artesian well of the Spirit that flows out everywhere we go. I believe this is only possible if we remain connected to the source, who is the fountain of living waters.

What is being released from your life these days? Are you gushing forth with the fresh river of life? My challenge to all of us is to stay attached to the source. Don't settle for anything else in your spiritual walk than an ongoing, intimate relationship with God. Don't settle for human attempts to hew cisterns to control or preserve His presence.

PRAYER

Father, forgive me for straying from you, the source of life. You are my fountain. You are the water of life. With your help I want to remain attached to you so that fresh streams of your Spirit will flow from my life, in Jesus' name, amen.

APPLICATION

1. How does this vision by Judy Franklin speak to you?
2. Do you tend to drift from the source of living water? Why or why not?
3. Are life-giving words or dull, stagnant words flowing out of you?
4. What are some things you can adapt or change in your life in order to keep the living water flowing in your life?

50

Trusting the Word

The moment we elevate our present reality over God's Word is the moment we start to formulate doctrines that fit the context of our experiences.

How much do you trust God's Word? Let me ask this another way: how much do you trust His Word when circumstances are contradictory to what His Word declares? No power is greater than His Word. Isaiah said that when God's Word is dispatched from His mouth, it will not return to Him empty (Isaiah 55:11). That literally means that His Word will always carry an effect. It simply cannot be dispatched and nothing happen. Think about creation and how the Spirit of God hovered over the surface of the waters. He was waiting with anticipation for one thing: the Word to be spoken. In the moment that God spoke, chaos became order.

Ezekiel encountered the same thing in a valley (Ezekiel 37:1–10). He looked and saw nothing but a dry heap of bones, and these bones were very dry indeed. This valley was a chaotic mess. Can these bones live again, God asked? Then Ezekiel prophesied over this dusty mess. He spoke God's Word over the situation, and an army arose out of the dry heap. Just imagine what could happen when God's Word is released over your circumstances.

In the New Testament it was an out-of-covenant Roman centurion who recognized the power of the Word. He came to Jesus because his servant was paralyzed and tormented (Matthew 8:6-8). Jesus offered to go and heal his servant, but the centurion refused because he didn't feel worthy of hosting Jesus in his home.

Then he said these unforgettable words to Jesus, "Just say the word, and my servant will be healed" (Matthew 8:8b). In other words, he realized that Jesus didn't need to be on the premises to heal someone. This centurion understood that Jesus' word carried such amazing authority that once it is released, it would fulfill its intended purpose. He had faith in the word of the Lord. He trusted the word over the circumstances that his servant was in. Jesus had never encountered faith like that, not even from His own disciples. Do you *really* believe the Word of the Lord?

What often happens to us is that our circumstances appear greater than the reality of His Word, and this opens the door to unbelief. The moment we elevate our present reality over God's Word is the moment we start to formulate doctrines that fit the context of our experiences. So, let me ask you again: do you trust His Word when circumstances are contradictory to what His Word declares?

There are people that I'm declaring healing over, but their circumstances have yet to change. Will I continue to declare God's Word over them or believe that my present reality trumps what He says? The Word makes strong declarations about healing. For example: "The prayer offered in faith will restore the one who is sick" (James 5:15a); "Heal the sick" (Matthew 10:8a); and Jesus said, ". . . He who believes in Me, the works that I do, he will do also" (John 14:12a). So, whose report will I believe? I don't have the authority to change God's Word. My only obligation is to trust what He says.

There are many other circumstances that are dry, chaotic, or even seem dead, but I'm speaking His Word over them. There are people bound by addictions, steeped in sin, overwhelmed by oppressions, and broken and far from God. I cannot, and I must not cease speaking God's Word over these situations because I believe His Word will prevail. I trust His Word even when I don't understand the circumstances because I believe there is power in what He says.

Mary was confronted by an angel of the Lord in Luke, and she was told that she would bear a Son of the Most High (Luke 1:31). Her circumstances prevented such a word from coming to pass because she was a virgin. But the angel of the Lord explained what would take place, and then he announced: "For nothing will be impossible with God" (Luke 1:37). The word "nothing" is translated "not any word." The angel was saying, "Not any word that God speaks will fail to come to pass."

Mary still wasn't sure how everything was going to transpire, but her lack of understanding didn't prevent her from

Trusting the Word

trusting what God said. "And Mary said, 'Behold, the bondslave of the Lord; may it be done to me according to your word'" (Luke 1:38). That should be our response in every situation we find ourselves in. Mary could have reasoned herself out of belief. She could have allowed her circumstances to undermine the declared Word of God, but she trusted His Word.

My encouragement to you is to trust the Word of God no matter where you might find yourself. Don't think that the mess you might find yourself in is the final word on the matter. Don't assume that things will always be the way that they are. You might be in a valley of dry bones, you might be hovering over chaos, or you might be in a barren situation with no hope in sight, but no word that God speaks will fail to come to pass. Time will not dissipate the strength of God's Word because there is no expiration date on the validity of what He says. "The grass withers, the flower fades, But the word of our God stands forever" (Isaiah 40:8).

Will you trust His Word over your circumstances?

PRAYER

God, your Word is eternal. Heaven and earth will pass away, but your Word will endure forever. Help me to trust what your Word says even when the circumstances in my life are contradictory to the Bible. I will not settle for anything less, amen.

APPLICATION

1. When difficult situations arise in your life, what is your first response?
2. Which usually reigns in your life as truth, His Word or your circumstances? Why?
3. What are some promises that you are trusting God for?
4. Attempt this week to make more time to spend in the Word, reading and studying truth. Make declarations from the Word over your life, instead of agreeing with lies from the world.

51

Resting in the Storm

Rest in the midst of conflict actually becomes a weapon that Jesus can use to bring redemption to those in bondage.

Jesus commissioned his disciples in Mark 4:35. It begins this way: "On that day, when evening came, He said to them, 'Let us go over to the other side.' Leaving the crowd, they took Him along with them in the boat, just as He was; and other boats were with Him" (Mark 4:35–36).

We have the luxury of knowing what was on the other side of the lake. The Bible indicates that there was a demon-possessed man who was transformed by Jesus. This man became the central vocal piece for the mercies of the Lord in Decapolis, an area that was steeped in sin, immorality, and humanism. That area was so "anti-Christ" that Jesus was all but forced out of their region when He first landed in the country of Gerasenes, in spite of the fact that a demon-possessed man was delivered.

Yet, as we learned, this redeemed man told people of Jesus, and they were amazed to the point that that next time Jesus traveled to the region, four thousand people were ministered to (Mark 8:1-9). Quite possibly one man's deliverance touched over four thousand people. So, when Jesus said, "Let's go over to the other side," citywide transformation was about to take place. You may never know what is on the other side of Jesus' call for your life until you obey Him. The challenge for you and me is to get to the other side!

After Jesus commissioned His disciples to go, they got in a boat and set sail. And then it happened—a fierce blast of wind kicked up the waves, which continuously beat the boat, and it began to fill with water. The Bible says that this mega-storm suddenly "arose" (Mark 4:37). This verb carries with it the idea of something suddenly happening without any warning.

I believe that it was a preemptive strike by the enemy to hinder the fulfillment of the commission of Jesus. Most scholars believe that this storm was not a natural one but a supernatural storm. It was something that was conjured up by the enemy. They call this a "demonic distraction" for the purpose of getting the disciples off course so that they wouldn't arrive on the other side.

Jesus' disciples were not the only ones commissioned, however. Every single person reading this has been commissioned by Jesus. Moreover, I believe that part of our call is to deliver people from demonic bondage (Mark 16:17). Jesus came to seek and save those who were lost (Luke 19:10), and He has commissioned us to do the same.

Resting in the Storm

Our call is to bring deliverance, hope, redemption, healing, and salvation to a lost and broken world. We are ministers of reconciliation who bring people to Christ (2 Corinthians 5:18-20). Think about this: every person that we touch, like the former demon-possessed man in Mark 5, is a potential candidate to bring citywide transformation. Our assignment from God is enormous . . . if we don't fall prey to the distractions that are sent to sink us.

This passage in Mark doesn't exactly describe what the disciples were doing when the storm started, but we know that they reacted in total fear (Mark 4:40). Their attention was drawn away from their commission, and it was captured by the enemy's tactics. They lost sight of Jesus' Word—let's go over to the other side, and they became focused on the demonic activity. It's no different when Jesus gives you an assignment and hell is stirred up against you in opposition. Will you lose sight of your call and become fearful in the face of difficulties?

It's essential to note what Jesus was doing during this demonic activity. The Bible says, "Jesus Himself was in the stern, asleep on a cushion" (Mark 4:38a). Jesus was resting in the storm because He trusted the Word spoken to Him by the Father. The Word indicated that they were going to the other side. Jesus placed confidence in what heaven declared; therefore, He rested in the Word rather than reacting to the enemy. The realm in which Jesus' mind was dwelling in possessed no storms. He was demonstrating what Paul later wrote, "Set your mind on the things above, not on the things that are on earth" (Colossians 3:2).

The truth is that we can generally count on the fact that Jesus' Word to us will be tested (Matthew 13:21). The Word of the Lord to Joseph was tested for thirteen years before it was fulfilled, yet he never lost sight of God's dream for him. You will be tested, but if you've died to yourself, then "keep seeking the things above, where Christ is, seated at the right hand of God" (Colossians 3:1b).

Actually, your redeemed position is to be seated in Him, in heavenly places (Ephesians 2:6). Don't become captivated with the enemy. Don't lose sight of your assignment to bring transformation to a world around you regardless of what the enemy stirs up. Learn to rest in your storms because in Christ you have the authority to speak "peace" over what threatens you. Your posture of rest next to Jesus is a threat to the kingdom of darkness because you're poised to move at the impulse of His voice. Rest, in the midst of conflict, actually becomes a weapon that Jesus can use to bring redemption to those in bondage.

Find your cushion the next time the enemy strikes. Keep your faith in the Word and fulfill your commission on the other side of that call. Let's bring the gospel of salvation to those in bondage without becoming distracted.

PRAYER

Jesus, you've called me to go and bring the good news to those in our communities. Don't let me become distracted when the enemy strikes. Help me to remain focused on things above and not on things of the earth, in your name, amen.

APPLICATION

1. Have you gotten up (just for a moment) from your position of authority seated in heavenly realms? Why or why not?
2. Do you typically live in rest or live in anxiety when circumstances come against you?
3. What are some ways that you can rest like Jesus did during adverse storms?
4. List the distractions that keep you from resting in your assignment. Take some time to give those distractions to Jesus and ask for His peace to fill your heart.

52

Believing Beyond Criticism

Believing God's Word will often put you in opposition with those around you who are overcome with fear and disbelief.

Have you heard of John Kirby or Alexander Garden? What about Bishop Lavington? There might be a few who recognize these men, but most would not. Perhaps you are familiar with Shaphat and Igal? Most likely, you are not. Interestingly, each of these individuals was a critic of their peers and generally, people don't remember critics. Sadly, some critics would not have any kind of ministry if they didn't live to criticize others.

Do you know who John Wesley and George Whitefield were? Most of us would recognize these two names because these men were prominent leaders of the eighteenth-century awakenings in England and America. They sacrificed much for the sake of the kingdom of God and the message of the gospel. Kirby, Garden, and Lavington, however, were the ministers who criticized Wesley and Whitefield and did everything possible to malign their ministries. Wesley and Whitefield didn't shrink back from their God-given assignments regardless of criticism. They believed beyond their critics.

Shaphat and Igal were two of the twelve spies who didn't believe God's Word or the favorable report given by two names that most of us would recall, Joshua and Caleb. Let's consider the details of their story. God came to Moses and said, "Send out for yourself men so that they may spy out the land of Canaan, which I am going to give to the sons of Israel, . . ." (Numbers 13:1a). Did you note that phrase God used? God had *already* promised to give Israel this territory. The spies were merely sent out to inspect the gift that was promised from God.

The Bible indicates that the spies came into the valley of Eshcol, which means a place of cluster or much blessing. In fact, these spies harvested a single cluster of grapes that took two men to carry (Exodus 13:23). After forty days, they returned home and proceeded to explain to Moses what they saw. They explained how the land flowed with milk and honey and they presented some of its fruit. Everything appeared to be going well, but then the unimaginable happened. Fear fell over the spies and they lost sight of God's promise. They focused on the size of the giants rather than the size of their God.

Two of the twelve, however, had a different perspective. They believed the report of the Lord. Caleb said, "We should by all means go up and take possession of it, for we will surely overcome it" (Numbers 13:30). The other ten were so convinced that taking the land couldn't happen, they began to spread a "bad report" among the Israelites (Numbers 13:32). This phrase means to spread a poisonous, slanderous word. It implies defaming the character of those with whom you disagree. Joshua and Caleb were being criticized for actually believing God's Word.

What about you? Believing God's Word will often put you in opposition with those around you who are overcome with fear and disbelief. They may criticize you, write things about you, leave your church, vote you out of the church, or worse, they may even try to physically harm you. The Israelites were so angered by the tenacious faith of Joshua and Caleb that they wanted to stone them (Numbers 14:10). The question is, however, will you still believe beyond the criticism?

If you become angry and offended, then you'll not respond in the correct manner. You don't need to harshly respond to critics or violently defend your reputation when people speak against you. Jesus said, "Blessed are you when people insult you and persecute you, and falsely say all kinds of evil against you because of Me" (Matthew 5:11). He actually said, "But I say to you who hear, love your enemies, do good to those who hate you, bless those who curse you, pray for those who mistreat you" (Luke 6:27–28). However, never shrink back from what you have been called to do and never stop believing God's Word.

Critics are a dime a dozen. They are everywhere and in every church. Most of them will not be remembered in history for igniting the fires of revival or sowing into great moves of God. They aren't known for what they believe as much as what they oppose. Usually, the hungrier you are for Jesus and the more desperate for the manifest presence of God that you become, the greater the criticism against you will be. If you place total faith in God's Word and little confidence in earthly circumstances, then you will become a target of criticism. Nevertheless, don't shrink back.

I like Paul's response to his critics when he was in Ephesus. He said, "I did not shrink from declaring to you the whole purpose of God" (Acts 20:27). He consistently preached the Word without relent regardless of the opposition that he faced. Not only was the Word of God heard throughout all of Asia, but a mighty revival exploded in the city of Ephesus that caused people to keep coming and confessing their sins and turning unto the Lord Jesus Christ (Acts 19:10–18).

So, no matter what, believe beyond the critics.

PRAYER

Jesus, regardless of who might come against me, I will not shrink back or cease believing your Word. Use me in any manner that you choose. I will believe beyond my critics, amen.

APPLICATION

1. Are there critics coming against you or your ministry? What is your attitude concerning them?
2. Why do you believe criticism is so prevalent? Do you criticize other people? If so, why?
3. Would you be willing to pray for those who criticize you?
4. Are you tempted to give up or quit because someone has criticized you? If so, why?

Other Books by Rob McCorkle

Bridging the Great Divide: Reuniting Word and Spirit

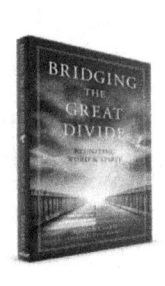

In this power-packed book, Dr. Rob McCorkle explains how the Word and the Spirit became separated and why people discount the supernatural. Without compromising the truths of God's Word, Rob calls all believers to a life of holiness while exploring how the supernatural power of the Holy Spirit should accompany one who is consecrated to Christ. Learn why biblical Christianity is the fusion of purity and power; the marriage of the Word with the Spirit. Discover anew Jesus' call to a lifestyle of intimacy with Him and how from that posture you can become a student of the Word and a practitioner of the Spirit. *Bridging the Great Divide* is a book that will both provoke and encourage you. As you journey through the Bible, history, theology, and practical stories, you will end up next to Jesus.

Holiness & Healing *(By Dan Bohi & Rob McCorkle)*

This book was inspired from a three hour interview where Dan candidly shared his personal journey. Rob and Dan both believe that the gospel is not a benign creed void of supernatural power, and neither do they believe it's incapable of fully redeeming the heart from all sin. They discuss in this book: God's calls to ordinary people to do extraordinary things, miraculous stories, divine encounters and supernatural manifestations, the place for God-called apostles and prophets in the Holiness movement, the ministries of healing and impartations, and hindrances to revival and how to sustain a kingdom culture. This book will inspire you and challenge your traditional thinking with profound biblical insights, and hopefully cause you to live and teach a message of holiness and healing.

Fire School Ministries
P.O. Box 511
Groveport, OH 43125
www.fireschoolministries.com

Notes

1. Quoted in W. T. Purkiser, *The Gifts of the Spirit* (Kansas City, MO: Beacon Hill Press, 1975), 73.
2. Rick Renner, *Sparkling Gems from the Greek* (Tulsa, OK: Teach All Nations, 2003), 526.
3. Ibid.
4. These thoughts were inspired by Brigid E. Herman, *Creative Prayer* (Cincinnati, OH: Forward Movement Publications, n.d.).
5. Rick Renner, *Dressed to Kill* (Tulsa, OK: Teach All Nations, 1991, 2007), 407.
6. Written by David Ruis.
7. Source unknown.
8. In 1988, in Kansas City, MO, I had the privilege to hear Ravenhill speak and then meet him after the service. It was a rare privilege that I'll always remember. His passion for prayer and revival in person was just the same as reading his books.
9. Ed Silvoso, *That None Should Perish* (Ventura, CA: Regal Books, 1994), 155.
10. Ibid.
11. Ramsay MacMullen, *Christianizing the Roman Empire A.D. 100-400* (London: Yale University Press, 1984).
12. Judy Franklin, contributing author, *Walking in the Supernatural* (Shippensburg, PA: Destiny Publishers, 2012), 209.